COMMON SENSE FOR A PROSPEROUS LIFE
BOOK 2

INVEST
LIKE A WEALTH MANAGER

Simplify Your Thinking to Invest
Your Money with Confidence

Mark Ashe

INVEST LIKE A WEALTH MANAGER © 2022, 2026
by Mark Ashe. All rights reserved.

Published by Author Academy Elite
PO Box 43, Powell, OH 43065
www.AuthorAcademyElite.com

All rights reserved. This book contains material protected under international and federal copyright laws and treaties. Any unauthorized reproduction, distribution, transmission, display, or use of this material is prohibited.

No part of this book may be reproduced or transmitted in any form or by any means, electronic or mechanical, including photocopying, recording, scanning, scraping, or by any information storage and retrieval system, without the express prior written permission of the author.

Without limiting the author's exclusive rights under copyright law, no part of this work may be reproduced, copied, extracted, scraped, ingested, analyzed, or used for the purpose of training, fine-tuning, developing, or improving artificial intelligence systems, machine learning models, or generative models—whether commercial or non-commercial—without the author's prior written consent.

The author expressly reserves all rights to license this work for any AI-related uses.

Identifiers:
LCCN: 2020922131
ISBN: 978-1-64746-598-8 (paperback)
ISBN: 978-1-64746-599-5 (hardback)
ISBN: 978-1-64746-600-8 (ebook)

Available in paperback, hardback, e-book

Scripture taken from the New King James Version®. Copyright © 1982 by Thomas Nelson. Used by permission. All rights reserved.

Cover designs by
Perry Yeldham, 21Thirteen Design, Inc.
perry@21thirteen.com
and
George Foster, Foster Covers
george@fostercovers.com

Other Books by Mark Ashe

The *Common Sense for a Prosperous Life* series

Riches Beyond the Bling
The Entry Level CEO
Unchain Your Brain
Private Choices, Public Power

Consider the little mouse, how sagacious an animal it is which never entrusts its life to one hole only.
—Plautus

CONTENTS

Author's Notes ix

Chapter 1—Protect The Money First 1
    What About a Professional? 4

Chapter 2—Sixth-Grade Math 7
    Why Save Money? 9
    Why Buy Stocks? 11
    Why Not Just Stocks? 15
    Buying Cheap 18
    Winning at Checkers 20

Chapter 3—Ground Rules For Intelligent Investing 22
    The Intelligent Investor 22
    Don't Be Sold 25
    Be Patient 27
    Plan Ahead 28

Chapter 4—The Plan: Where To Invest 31
    Cash 31
    Gold and Silver 32

Stocks 35

Real Estate. 36

Speculation 39

Chapter 5—The Plan: Sticking To It 41

Making It Easy 41

Who's in Control? 42

Keep It Simple. 43

Chapter 6—The Plan: Managing It 46

Keep Mistakes Small 46

Being in Control 49

Chapter 7—The Plan: Speculation. 53

A Simple Test for Speculative Investment Decisions. 54

What You Need to Be Able to Do. 56

Learning Patience 58

Examples. 59

Example: 1990. 60

Example: Around 1993 61

Immediate Inconvenience 62

Example: 1998. 63

Example: 2003. 63

Don't Get Greedy 64

Example: 2008. 66

An Expanded Checklist 68

    Your Questions 69

    Wait and Be Contrary 70

    Bottom Line 72

Chapter 8—More Hard-Won Tips. 73

    Small Deals Can Make Money Safely 74

    The Most Common Cause of the "Big Loss" . . .75

    Keep an Investment Journal 78

    One More Time: Don't Get Greedy 84

Chapter 9—Wisdom Keys. 87

    One More Thing: Stewardship 96

    How Will You Die? 99

Chapter 10—Play Life To Win, Play Money Not
          To Lose 101

    Courage to Live without Regret 101

    Safeguarding Your Money and Your Life. . 103

    In Summary 105

    My Story Can Be Yours 109

Appendix 1 – The Truth About Inflation 115

Appendix 2 – Bonds And Limited Partnerships 117

About the Author 119

AUTHOR'S NOTES

As I sit in my study, I am looking at a framed photograph of Orison Swett Marden. Mr. Marden wrote a lot in the late 1800s about character and its relationship to wealth. He was orphaned as a young boy and put out to hard labor as little more than a slave. Overworked and underfed, he was often beaten by a tyrannical master. Half-starving most of the time, he would sneak an extra bite of food when he found it, terrified of the beating he would receive if he were caught. With no one to aid him, encourage him, guide him—or even love him—he yet *lifted himself* to become one of the preeminent authors of his time. He wrote with authority on the subject of rising from limiting circumstances to achieve a satisfying place in life.

After submitting his first book, *Pushing to the Front,* to several publishers—unsure if any would be willing to print it—to his surprise, publishers actually fought each other over the rights to the book. That book was reprinted again and again and distributed around the globe! Governments bought the book for nationwide distribution in their schools.

In a later book, *Good Manners: A Passport to Success*, Mr. Marden penned twenty-seven words that set the course of my adult life:

> **It is the duty of every young person, and especially of every young man, to set about the task of becoming financially independent. The amount is inconsequential.**

From the first time I read those words, now thirty-five years ago, those two sentences became my personal philosophy—and my obsession. They became my life's field manual and I began a passionate pursuit to attain financial independence.

Even though I still am not a financial sophisticate or a business tycoon (or even had those things as goals), by the age of forty-five I lived on a beautiful farm in the foothills of the North Georgia mountains and I was debt-free and financially independent. My wife and children were living a blessed life, and I was there with them to enjoy every day of it.

Armies issue their new soldiers a "field manual." When faced with a decision, a soldier can go to the manual, refer to the appropriate section, and see quickly what to avoid and what course of action to take to increase the odds of a desirable outcome. I have long been of the opinion that, if a practical reference manual could be written for making the major decisions of life—especially if written in an engaging style—a great need would be met for us civilians fighting the battles of life.

To that end, I have written the Common Sense for a Prosperous Life book series, five quick-read handbooks that cut straight to the heart of the most important issues of life:

1. earning and spending,
2. saving and investing,
3. running a business,

AUTHOR'S NOTES

4. creative thinking, intention, and focus, and
5. mature judgment, marriage, and other personal choices.

But I chose to write these books—including the one you now hold in your hand—with great reluctance. Here's how it happened.

In 2008 I witnessed the global financial meltdown that would shake the world's markets for years, but I had seen it coming. Almost all of the "prosperity" everyone seemed to be enjoying leading up to the crash was an illusion built on excessive debt and other bad decisions.

During those earlier years of society-wide excessive borrowing and spending, an unbidden idea kept pushing itself up, forcing its way into my mind. The thought seemed preposterous, an errant notion passing through the wrong mind, and, at first, I treated it exactly like that. Over time, however, it grew into a conviction that I could not escape, even as I continued to thrust it away.

Here is that thought:

> Mark, *you* write a book that will give the reader a healthy foundation for decisions concerning money, business, and personal life. This current foolishness—the "You can get rich quick and live rich now; here's how!" mantra being fed to the unsophisticated and gullible public by new money magazines, how-I-got-rich authors, and breathless news anchors on financial channels excitedly reporting the day's Wall Street winners—must be confronted.
>
> The healthy intention to become an independent, balanced, self-restrained adult has been lost. Independence, not consumption, must once again be held up for all to see as the proper purpose of labor. *You* are to write a book that will spell out, in simple terms, a practical mindset

toward money, business, and life that will provide a road map to help ordinary men and women see clearly to make wiser choices.

As I have said, I repeatedly dismissed this most unwelcome impulse. After many years of hard work in my own business, I had no appetite for such a time-consuming task, nor did I feel competent. Not only did I feel unqualified to write about these things—after all, my accomplishments are modest when compared to those of the wealthy best-selling authors so prevalent on bookshelves—but I did not believe I had any gift at all for writing, on *any* subject. I did not want, nor have I ever desired, to write a book.

For several years, I continued to consider the thought ridiculous. Then I had a health scare that turned out to be a false alarm. But this was the turning point for me. Why? Because the first thought that went through my mind when I feared bad news was not for myself or my family. To my shock, it was instead, "I should have written that book."

That's when I realized this work was something I *must* do, I was *intended* to do, whether or not I thought it reasonable. And even before I returned the call to the doctor's office, I made up my mind that I would begin.

In 2010—after nearly a decade of my hard work—*Your Money & Your Life: A Guide to Building Character and Capital* was published. The feedback I got was that it was fantastic, but so varied in topics and filled with good information that it would've been helpful to be more subject-specific.

So, I went back to work for a few more years, and now you have in your hand the result—one volume in a five-book series called *Common Sense for a Prosperous Life*. One way or another, the writing of these books has taken much of my time for nearly eighteen years, and, at this moment, I still have no idea if this series will ever see the light of day. But I do know

AUTHOR'S NOTES

this much: books such as these are needed *badly*, and, if these books are ever published, everyone who reads them will be better off because they will finish every book with far greater clarity of thought for decision making on the subjects that determine quality of life.

Only a fortunate few are born into this world with a "wealth consciousness"—a mind that expects or creates wealth—or gifted with a highly marketable talent. The rest of us have to devote a great deal of our time to earning money and deciding how our very limited resources should be used. The Common Sense for a Prosperous Life series was written to give just this sort of reader a mature and sensible mindset toward all kinds of money matters, and also a blueprint for conquering our private demons and making personal choices that are as clear as "Follow the yellow brick road."

Let me begin by stating the obvious. For all but the truly wealthy, building a comfortable life will require several things:

- You must handle whatever you earn deliberately, so it does not slip away.

- You must earn more money than is required for food, clothing, shelter, and other living expenses (which, I admit, is increasingly difficult to do).

- You must not be careless with the money you save.

- You must overcome your own internal hindrances.

- You must not forfeit your progress to an undisciplined private life.

By the time you have finished reading this series, you will have a road map for the five "musts" above.

Book 1—*Riches Beyond the Bling: Clear Thinking on Money, Financial Independence and Life's True Riches* reveals how to handle the money you earn, purposefully.

Book 2—*Invest Like a Wealth Manager: Simplify Your Thinking to Invest Your Money with Confidence* gives you my own common-sense guidelines for saving and investing.

Book 3—*The Entry-Level CEO: Simple Secrets to Build a Profitable Business (Even with No Experience!)* is ideal for those with a desire to work for themselves. It relates some thoughts on increasing your income by building a business of your own.

Book 4—*Unchain Your Brain: Move Beyond Fear and Discouragement and Start Living with Purpose* delivers a powerful read for overcoming fear and discouragement and moving you toward your next goal.

Book 5—*Private Choices, Public Power: Personal Decisions that Determine Your Destiny* is the fifth and final book in the series, is filled with practical help regarding personal issues, which, if handled carelessly, can wreck a life.

None of these books is a sermon, and they are not boring—I promise. I believe every page will grip you with its practical and immediate common sense. Pick up any of the books, open them anywhere, read three pages, and I trust you will not want to quit reading from right where you are. To my mind, that is the test of a well-written and worthy book: there is no place in it that does not quickly engage the reader on a personal level.

The lessons contained within are timeless. They will be just as helpful to a reader sixty years from now as today. So, if you are a parent and you can read this book without considering it imperative to set aside a copy for each of your children, I have

AUTHOR'S NOTES

failed. If you are a wife and you can read this book without insisting that your husband also read it, I have failed.

I truly believe you will not toss these aside: I am *that* confident that the five books in the *Common Sense for a Prosperous Life* series have no substitute in the marketplace. Having read hundreds of such books myself, I believe these are among those rare works immediately useful to every reader in every generation.

Welcome into my major life assignment, my best effort to make the world a better place by giving the reader practical instruction for the most important issues of life.

Choose well and prosper.

Mark Ashe
Gainesville, Georgia
2020

CHAPTER 1
PROTECT THE MONEY FIRST

Invest Like a Wealth Manager is not about becoming a shrewd capitalist. It is a practical course on how to apply common sense before you part with your cash.

Writing words on paper does not make any author an expert. As I read and read again the words I have written trying to make this series the best it can be, it occurs to me that anyone writing this book ought to have made much more money than I have.

If you have read any of the other books in my Common Sense for a Prosperous Life series, you'll already be familiar with the rough outline of my life and my education—or rather the lack of it—in how to handle money.

But, just in case, here's a quick refresher: I was a law enforcement specialist (base policeman) in the United States Air Force. After I finished out my enlistment, I took a job as a civilian police officer back in my home state of Georgia, all the while trying to think of some way to go into business.

When I did leave police work, I found myself in a business for which I was poorly suited. The next sixteen years were filled by exhausting and unsatisfying labor, with no apparent way to escape.

Still—though at quite a price—I finally earned many of the material things we all start out after. In other words, with little more in the way of qualifications than a lot of persistence and some common sense—no college education, no special training—I eventually became financially independent—though it took twenty-six years from when the thought first occurred to me. I had no advantages other than some basic common sense, a fierce determination to live free from debt, and an unshakable commitment to be in business for myself. That was enough for me to become independent by my mid-forties.

Then, in 2010, I had serious reversals come upon me unexpectedly, as did many during those years, and they threatened the loss of everything I had earned to that point. These were business losses, not investment mistakes, and I had plenty of investment blunders in my history as well.

It took most of what I had to straighten things out, but, afterward, much to my relief, I still owned my home and my business, even though I had less money to show for all those years of hard work. (Had I not taken steps to protect my family's necessities first, and then set aside something for emergencies with my earnings of many years up to that point, I doubt I would have come out intact. You might want to read *Riches Beyond the Bling*, the first book in this series, to see that financial plan.)

I never bemoaned the financial losses. I was thankful I had the means to survive the setback.

Regarding investing, I have had private conversations with men and women a lot wealthier and a lot smarter than me. To my surprise, they had made my same investing mistakes exactly, and for exactly the same reasons. So, if you ever have more than enough money for basic needs, or come into a little money and start thinking, "What can I do with this money to make more money with it," … well, that thought is fraught with financial danger, and this book was written for you. There is no need for every generation to keep making the same costly blunders.

As you read in my *Author's Notes* to you—please read it now, if you haven't already—I felt called to write about my experiences in order to help others avoid my mistakes and learn from my successes and failures.

And one of the topics I felt needed attention was saving and investing—*intelligent* investing—for the ordinary person. So, this book was written for the many of us who start with nothing and must avoid major mistakes so that we can put aside enough to be independent or qualify for the services of a professional money manager.

The best thing an average person can do with money is either remain steady with a simple long-term plan or be in agreement with the methods of a detached pro, this book should help you with both.

My goal with *Invest Like a Wealth Manager* is to help you to protect what you have first, which is how a wealth manager thinks, so you can avoid common and costly errors. Hopefully, your growing knowledge will lead to your own independence or your resources will eventually qualify you for the services of a professional money manager.

How does a wealth manager think? First, remember I am talking about those who manage assets for the wealthy—not about stockbrokers. To explain further, a retail stockbroker makes his money by buying and selling stocks for others, often recommending the ones that benefit the brokerage firm. A good broker can be a great asset. I have friends that have benefitted from their brokers' advice for years. But stockbrokers want their recommendations to meet or beat market averages. A wealth manager thinks in terms of an overall plan, and their top priority is protecting the money.

Wealth managers are men and women who may allocate dollars across many major asset classes. For example, stocks, bonds, commodities, real estate, etc., and they often act contrary to the prevailing trend when doing so. Their thinking and investing are done first and foremost to keep the clients accumulated assets safe.

With that in mind, I will assume that I have been asked to write on this subject: "How Not to Lose All Your Money to Inexperience, Gullibility, or a Market Crash until You Can Make Your Own Financial Decisions Intelligently and with Confidence"—because that is exactly what this book amounts to.

What About a Professional?

In 2010, as I explained in the Author's Notes, I released *Your Money & Your Life* in which much of this same material was presented. However, I have come to different conclusions on several important issues in the intervening years and have updated my views in this new book series.

Most important, in the earlier book I suggested that a professional investment manager was unnecessary if one simply waited to invest when a crash made assets cheap. In the years since I have come to believe this advice simply does not work with human nature. Most people that come into or save money cannot long resist the temptation to try to do something profitable with it. And therein lies the danger.

If one invests a little out of each paycheck there is a certain amount of safety since deposits are added slowly over a course

> To earn money is difficult enough, but investing it safely is even more difficult, much more.

of years. But I have noticed that when people come into sums of money—perhaps an inheritance or a retirement payout—they suddenly feel compelled to do more with it than they are capable of doing.

That is exactly the time professional management is most needed. Trying to do something smart and profitable because one now has more money to invest will, in the vast majority of instances, only lead to pain and loss. **The correct motive in investing is always to protect the money first**—a lesson I learned, like most, only after expensive losses.

To earn money is difficult enough, but investing it safely is even more difficult, much more. Everyone thinks they understand what the word "safe" means, but very few know what it looks like when investing money.

However, there are men and women with the skills and temperament and training to invest money according to a sound plan. If one has enough money to qualify for their services, I am now certain that it is best to let those professionals do what they are good at.

Again, I am referring to a professional manager of wealth—and one with a proven track record long enough to have been through at least two serious bear markets. Financial planners and accountants can also be consulted, and decisions made after considering the guidance offered by each.

You could also just buy income, such as rental property, if you have enough money for that. After all, you can't go far wrong owning anything debt-free that will give you an income for life and that you can sell at will. This is what I consider the safest course, and it is my preference for my own money.

If you already have a good bit of money or if you come into a large sum of money in the future, I suggest you find a pro you are comfortable working with. Reading this book will aid greatly in helping the two of you talk and think in the same language. If this is your situation then make this your mutual goal:

> *I want you to protect this money from my inexperience and from 100 percent exposure to market crashes and prepare a reasonable plan for growth or income long-term.*

Successful investing is not a series of profitable individual decisions, but an overarching plan that will work over time. Of course, no one knows what is going to happen short-term. Even with a pro's help, account values will rise and fall sharply at times. Understanding and sticking with a sound plan *is* the safety net.

And here's another advantage to using the services of a trusted counselor: living without the mental preoccupation of what to do with invested money makes life much more enjoyable.

Whether you want to learn to act on your own financial behalf with greater confidence or use a professional wealth manager, read on for some truly valuable suggestions, almost all learned from my own mistakes.

Invest Like a Wealth Manager is not about becoming a shrewd capitalist. It is a practical course on how to apply common sense before you part with your cash. It is about learning how to invest intelligently so you don't lose those dollars faster than you can save them.

I endured some agonizing losses to learn these truths. I hope this book will save you from some of that pain.

CHAPTER 2
SIXTH-GRADE MATH

Why do you and mom try to save money?

This may sound strange, but I think the best place to begin a discussion of intelligent saving and investing is to share with you a conversation I had with my daughter Scarlett many years ago while she and I were going over her grade-school math lesson.

The lesson involved finding the return with various rates of interest, and she asked me to explain interest. I said:

> In this lesson interest is the money paid to you by the bank for the use of your money. When you put money into a bank, they loan that money out to other people and make a profit for the bank with it. They pay depositors a little interest so they can attract deposits and operate the bank.
>
> Scarlett, in this problem posed to you, you see that $5,000 placed in a bank at 6 percent simple interest will earn you an additional $300 in one year's time. So, at the end of a year, you will have $5,300 in the bank. However, this is not all you

must consider. You and I have talked about inflation, the term used for the falling value of money. [See more on this topic in Appendix 1.]

As the government spends more than it takes in through taxes, it must borrow or print more money to cover the shortfall. Governments have always done this whenever their ability to print paper money was not limited by the amount of gold they were required to hold to support it.

Paper money is called currency. Most nations have their own or share with other nations a mutual currency, and, since currency—what we loosely refer to as money—is no longer backed by anything of objective real value, governments are free to print as much of it as they desire since they are not limited by how much gold or other acceptable stores of value they have.

But all that new paper money every year makes the nation's currency—in our case, dollars—constantly worth less.

Scarlett asked, "Why, Daddy?"
I explained,

> As more and more dollars are created to pay for government spending, each individual dollar has a little less value, and it takes more of them to buy something. It's kind of like when you were little and your mother added water to your grape juice. The juice is still in there, but it is weaker because it has been diluted.
>
> So, let's take this real-life lesson about money and apply it to your school math problem. In this

example, you have earned $300 interest in a year. However, the rate of inflation this year is around 8 percent, though the government does not admit that because it makes them look bad. With an 8 percent inflation rate, in one year your $5,000 will lose $400 in the amount of things it will buy.

To buy the same amount of things with it in one year, you will need to have $5,400 instead of $5,000. In your example, the $5,000 you put in the bank will be $5,300 in one year. You will have more money, as $5,300 is more than $5,000, but you have actually lost $100 worth of what your savings will buy for you.

This happens each year, and it is the reason why the $14,000 house that I grew up in forty years ago now costs $225,000. It is not that the home is worth that much more; it is just that it takes much more paper money to buy it because the money is worth less. That is why real estate is considered a good investment. Over long periods of time, it tends to benefit from inflation.

Why Save Money?

Scarlett then asked, "Then why do you and mom try to save money? Why not buy a house with it?"
   I said,

> That's a good question. The reason is that it takes money to buy the things we need, like food and clothing. And it takes money to solve the problems that come up unexpectedly, like car repairs.
>
> So, you want to always save a percentage of what you earn and set it aside, just as your mother and

> I have you do now. People have a duty to themself to have some money saved. You want to keep saving until you have enough cash on hand to live on for a while or to pay for unexpected expenses.
>
> After that, buying land or a building or a home that you can rent to someone is a good idea. But save some cash first.

"Dad, how does it work when you rent to someone? What does that mean?"

> Well, you know Mr. Ray who I rent the blue house to, right? Mr. Ray does not want to buy a house. He just wants to have a place to stay when he is in our town working. He pays me $875 a month to use one of the homes I own. That money he pays me to use my home is called rent.
>
> That home is not quite paid for yet. I still have to pay the bank $675 a month for what I owe them on the home until it is paid for. So, Scarlett, let me ask you this: whose money is really paying for that home?

"Mr. Ray's," she said.
I said,

> That's right, Scarlett. I used the money I borrowed from the bank, which is called credit, to buy that home, and Mr. Ray pays for it.
>
> The money I owe the bank for the home is called debt. That's what debt is for: to pay for things that create wealth. Debt should not be used to buy things you want. You do that with cash.

Now, as that home goes up in value over the years, since I own it, who will that benefit? Mr. Ray or me?

"You," she said.

"Correct! And if I sell that home for a lot more money later, who does that benefit? Him or me?"

"You!"

"Right again. And it gets even better. The government lets me deduct the interest I pay the bank and a small amount of the home's value from the taxes I owe them each year. Who does that benefit?"

"You, again!"

> Yes, and you are right again! And banks are in business to loan you money to buy real estate. They will also let you borrow money against the real estate if it is worth more than you owe the bank for it.
>
> You see, real estate is very different from stocks. Stocks don't have to go up with inflation. They can go up or down—a lot! And you have to pay taxes on stocks as soon as you sell them. If I sell real estate for a profit and buy more investment real estate with the money, I can delay paying taxes on the profits. For these reasons, real estate has advantages over some other investments.

Why Buy Stocks?

"It sounds like real estate is a lot better than stocks. Why would you ever buy stocks, Dad?"

> Because, Scarlett, there is no perfect investment. Real estate is not a perfect investment, and neither

are stocks. They are just different. They may each have a place to help you.

The stocks I own can be sold and the money put into my account within three minutes of calling my broker and telling him to sell them. Real estate can't be sold so quickly.

Right now, we have a friend at church who has found this out the hard way. You know him, so I won't tell you his name. He bought a big home to live in because he thought it would make him money as it went up in value. Later, he bought a second home to rent. His business has slowed down, as has everyone's this year, and, at the same time, his renter moved out. He can't pay for both homes. In fact, because of his business slowing down, right now he can't pay for either.

And because his income is down and the value of homes has been falling, the bank won't loan him any more money. In fact, the banks have so much money tied up in troubled real estate loans that some don't have any money to lend. This is rare, but it can happen, and it is happening now.

Our friend has been trying to sell his homes for two years so he can buy a smaller one he can afford to live in, but there are just no buyers for homes right now. He is in real trouble. Soon the bank may have to take his homes. If this happens, his family will have no place to live. He is under so much pressure that it is affecting his health.

So, you can see why I would not want to have *all* my money in something that cannot be sold quickly. In a financial crisis, that can be like having no money at all. Do you see that?

"Yes, I do. Wow! I'm glad you have not put all our money into that."

And, Scarlett, never have all your wealth tied up in the home you live in either. When I said, "Do not ever have all your money invested in something that makes the money hard to get to," that includes your home.

The house you live in is not an investment, though it will probably be worth more than you paid for it when you sell it. It is an expense, a *liability*. A liability is anything that costs you money, and, as you know, it costs a lot of money to pay for and furnish and keep up a home. So, don't tie up all your money in a nice house; it's just not worth it. Everyone wants a beautiful home. But life is much more fun when you have some free money, even if your home is not as nice as you would prefer.

Once your mother and I were out of debt, I wanted to set aside a good bit of money, and I wanted it invested in something that could be quickly converted to cash, but also have a chance to grow, since I may never need it. How quickly you can get an investment changed back into cash is called *liquidity*. A *liquid* investment means you have invested your money in such a way that the money can flow back to you quickly, just like water. Everyone should have a portion of their investments in something liquid, like stocks.

The best guide is that it should be enough to make you feel comfortable. For your mother and me, I try to keep some of our money in cash and some in stocks. As I mentioned, you should never have all your money in real estate or in anything else that makes the money hard to access. No one should ever have all their money tied up in a way that makes it hard to get to in an emergency—*not even in good investments.*

And try never to have all your money tied up in only one investment. If that one thing doesn't work out, it could take all your money away with it. Life is full of uncertainties, and it is impossible to be prepared for everything that could happen, no matter how careful you are. My advice: don't have all your money at risk at any one time. No matter what you invest in, always hold some cash.

Do you understand these things I'm explaining?

"Yes, I do," she said.
With that assurance, I continued,

> Let's go back to what we learned with your original math lesson. How do I protect dollars that are losing a little of their value each year, but still be able to get the cash quickly if I need it? How do I protect that money from inflation instead of simply leaving it in a bank to slowly dwindle away in value?
>
> As you know, your mother and I have a savings account to cover household emergencies and a checking account to pay for living expenses. But with those accounts, we don't have to be concerned about inflation. A few thousand dollars to cover emergencies is just not enough money to be concerned about the effects of inflation, and the checking account money is going to be spent.

Besides, those monies are supposed to be held in cash.

But since I may not ever need my liquid investment fund, what do I do with it? Where do I put the portion of my investment money I want to keep liquid, so it can grow but still be where I can get to it as quickly as cash? That is when the stock market is helpful. Are you following me so far? Do you want me to continue?

"Yes. It's interesting!"

All right. Good! So, if something really unexpected happened, like an accident or the temporary slowdown of my business—something that required more than a few thousand dollars to get through it—and all my money was in real estate, I could be in trouble. Unless the real estate was worth a lot more than I owed for it; then I could borrow money against it, as long as the economy was okay and the banks were willing.

But, if some of my money were in stocks, I could make one phone call and turn the stocks into cash. This is one of the reasons stocks are useful. They can be sold very quickly. And stocks generally rise in value over longer periods of time. So, even though all stocks go up and down day to day, over time they can give you some protection from inflation because, as companies grow, their stock shares become more expensive.

Why Not Just Stocks?

"Then why not just buy stocks?" she asked.

Because there are risks—serious risks—to owning stocks. Since stock values are quoted minute by minute, their price is subject to the changing emotions of the people buying and selling them. Something can happen to make everyone fearful and stocks can go down quickly. This is the risk you take in order to have immediate access to your money.

Real estate can also go up or down in value. But it almost never happens fast because real estate cannot be sold "on demand." A company can have difficulties or go out of business completely and its stock will no longer have value. However, land is permanent. A building or a home is a physical property that always has some value. There is always a need for them at some price. And, as money falls in value, it takes more of it to buy these things.

Any company can go broke or have a scandal, and, if you own stock in that company, your investment will suddenly be worth much less. If you own a large group of stocks, you are safer, but there can still be wide swings in prices. For these reasons, I think you should not have all your money in the stock market, even though you can get to the money invested there very easily.

And, Scarlett, you should never use borrowed money to buy stocks. This is another way stocks are very different from real estate.

There are other problems with stocks, too. Companies can report how much money they make in a way that is not quite truthful. Also, the men and women who make their living on Wall Street selling a company's stock will only tell you the good news, especially when they are talking on television. They usually want to minimize the possibility that anything bad might happen. There are many ways men and women inside the stock-selling business can make a company's stock sell for more money than it is worth. In fact, that very thing is the business of Wall Street.

Fortunately, you can buy large groups of stocks instead of just the stock of one company. That way, if just one or two companies have a problem, it won't affect your investment much. Mutual funds or exchange-traded funds are easy ways for people to buy groups of stocks.

But even when buying groups of stocks, the money you invest can go down for a while. Sometimes by quite a lot. For that reason, it is best not to have any money in the stock market that you might need in the next five years. And, unless you are buying stocks regularly with some of your monthly income, it is safest to wait to buy your stocks until after some panic has made them cheap. This may happen only once every seven or eight years.

The stock market is the only place I know of where bargain prices scare buyers away. When prices are high and rising higher, people get excited and want to put their money in. They think they are missing out on easy profits. But the more exciting the news is and the higher the prices are when you buy, the more risk you have because the stocks have already gone up. The lower the prices are when you buy, as long as the business is sound, the less risk you have.

When everyone else has been selling for a while, all the news will be very bad and it will feel scary to buy, but that is the safest time and the smartest. So, if you ever decide you want to put a lump sum of money into the stock market and leave it there, it is best to hold that money in cash—even for years if necessary—and then buy only after everyone else has been scared away by falling prices.

This would not be a consideration, however, if you are making regular contributions to the stock market. When you grow up and are earning your own money and simply investing a portion out of each paycheck in stocks, then just keep investing when prices fall, rather than wish you had never invested in stocks at all.

Buying Cheap

"Dad, why doesn't everyone just wait to buy when things are cheap?"

> Because immature investors are too impatient to do this. As soon as they have some money, they want to invest in something, especially if the market is hot with rising prices. Mature investors are very patient. They only part with their money when there is very little risk and a strong probability of gain.
>
> Although I have done a lot of things right financially, this has been the hardest thing for me to learn. Once I was out of debt and actually had to make decisions concerning when and where

to invest, I made mistakes. That is how I learned what I'm teaching you now.

When a lot of people seem to be making money, it's hard to remain on the sidelines and await a real opportunity, one that you thoroughly understand and know is right. That is why it is helpful to find a mentor, and I will be yours. Unless you are putting a set amount into stocks every time you get paid, you need to learn to wait patiently and buy only when something goes on sale, even when you have money ready to invest. You will learn this better after a few mistakes of your own but listening to a wise friend and learning from his or her mistakes can help a lot. Do you understand this?

"Yes, Dad, I do," she said.

Scarlett, a perfect investment is one in which there is no risk to your money, you get high profits, and you can change your investment to cash right away if you need to. That investment does not exist. It never has and it never will.

You will hear stories of such investment opportunities many times in your life, often on television or from an excited friend, but trust me daughter: no matter how convincing the story sounds, it is just another con artist selling snake oil. And since there is no perfect investment and no one knows what will happen tomorrow, there is always a need to hold some cash, and there is a place for real estate when you can afford it, and stocks—if you are patient. And owning some gold of your own is always a good idea, too. Owning gold just sounds like fun, doesn't it? So, one kind of investment may not be "better" than another, just different. And they all have their place. But that is enough about money for today.

Winning at Checkers

Then I asked, "What do you think?"

Scarlett answered, "It reminds me of a checkerboard."

She lost me there. And, I want to tell you, I almost panicked! I thought, *Oh no! I've just done all this explaining of critical life lessons, and it has all gone right over her head.* So, I paused for a moment to collect myself and then calmly asked, "How so, Scarlett? How does it remind you of a checkerboard?"

She said, "You have to make the right moves or you can lose your men to play the game with."

Her insight overwhelmed me. "Yes! Scarlett, that's it exactly." Since she seemed to be keeping up, I continued the conversation for just a little longer.

> And Scarlett, it is not as hard to make the right moves as it seems. You just need some simple rules you can easily understand and follow. That way it is easier to make good decisions and harder to get off course.
>
> There will always be experts—people who are very gifted in some aspect of investing—who don't need to follow such simple guidelines as I have just given you. And the problem is, they can be very convincing when they explain how anyone can do what they do. In fact, quite a few of them write books making that very claim. But usually, that's just not so. Becoming an expert at anything takes dedication and time and a certain natural flair for the activity.

So, keep in mind: my rules are good for most people, but not everyone. Still, it is best to follow simple rules unless and until, you too become much more experienced at some particular field of investing. Remember, unless you become an expert at something, and probably even then, never have all your money in any one investment.

Scarlett, here is how I use my men on the checkerboard, as you so cleverly put it. I keep a portion of my money in cash, part in gold and silver, some in real estate, and some in stocks, and I reserve some of it for rare, unexpected opportunities. And I try to buy those things only when they appear to be cheap at the time. You should learn to be perfectly content to do nothing but accumulate cash until that happens.

There is a lot of common sense in that conversation I had with my oldest daughter, isn't there? **Thrift and savings are how homes and families are made strong, and it is no different for businesses or nations.**

CHAPTER 3
GROUND RULES FOR INTELLIGENT INVESTING

Avoid the three most common reasons for a permanent loss of capital.

Let us now take my view of commonsense, intelligent investing beyond the sixth-grade level, and examine some specifics. I want to offer you a few simple ground rules that may save you much anguish and loss. But first, what do I mean by intelligent investing?

The Intelligent Investor

What do most of us do that so often results in the loss of our money? We get a few dollars and start looking for some hot stock or other investment to grow our meager pile of cash. We—and I include myself as I too was guilty—start trying to catch lightning in a bottle with our few dollars.

GROUND RULES FOR INTELLIGENT INVESTING

I can define an intelligent investor in one sentence:

*An investor becomes an **intelligent** investor when he or she invests in strict accord with a predetermined plan.*

Much more on how to put together that plan soon, but let's start with a few basics. The plan does not need to be complicated. My former neighbor did very well by putting aside a portion out of each paycheck for forty years. He put one-third of his weekly savings into a stock fund, one-third into a bond fund, and one-third into government bonds, which in those years were paying 5 percent. He told me, "People get into trouble fooling with their money. The pros don't even agree from one week to the next, and I know they are smarter than me. So, I just did it that way for forty years. My friends ridiculed me for being so simple, but it sure worked!"

He had a plan, he stuck with it, he lived within his means, and he refused temptations to stray or stop when profits looked easier elsewhere or when pundits were predicting the end of the financial world.

He proves an important point:

Intelligent investing does not imply that you understand complicated methods of investment.

It simply means all your investments are intelligent choices **for you** because *you understand what you are buying and why you are buying it* and, therefore, can exercise prudential control over your own actions. In other words, an intelligent investor refuses to listen to "tips" and refuses to do anything with his or her money that is not fully understood.

My investment path did not take the preferred route of starting young and keeping to it. Being self-employed and having no predictable monthly paycheck, I paid off debts with any money I could save in case my business failed. Once my income began to improve, I remained determined to get out of debt. My mind was already set in that direction, so I just kept at it.

In my forties, when I finally started investing in earnest, I did not have the money to qualify for professionally managed accounts. I was debt-free but did not have much saved. I felt I was starting a bit late to simply "ride the market," and interest rates being paid on bonds at the time were near zero, so I took matters into my own hands, with regrettable results. Almost all that fills this book are the lessons I learned the expensive way.

I am not a financial savant; so don't scour these pages looking for a quick way to wealth. You won't find it. As they say, when a man with money but no experience meets a man with experience and no money, the man with the experience gets the money—and the man who used to have the money gets some "experience". I am the guy that got some experience.

But the errors of another are the best guideposts on earth. Therefore, I urge you to consider well what I learned from my follies. Use what helps; lay aside whatever does not suit you. My many losses made me more cautious. What follows in these pages are the considerations I use to weigh an investment today.

Remember: readers who already qualify for a professionally managed account should consider using a pro. My advisor is a genuine professional with over forty years of full-time experience in the battle for investment survival, and he requires only $50,000 to open an account. So, the threshold for professional help is not as high as one might suspect.

However, for a pro really to have something to work with, he or she will reasonably need at least three or four times that much in today's dollar values.

And remember again: by "professional," I do not mean a retail broker who will take your money and put it in the stock market. I learned from my advisor—a chief investment strategist for a national brokerage firm—that a pro should have a tactical plan to react to interest rate changes and unanticipated events.

He or she should also have the ability to take contrarian positions to profit from reversals in stock or bond prices. This allows you to benefit when conditions are favorable, and perhaps even when they aren't, but also allows for a quick "flight to safety" when called for.

These are things an individual with a normal career outside the money business is not able to do on their own.

However, as promised, there are a few simple ground rules for intelligent investing you can follow as you build toward the time when you can entrust your wealth to an expert.

Here are my three.

Don't Be Sold

1. Intelligent investing does not ever involve having something sold to you.

Intelligent investing—by definition—precludes participating in any financial arrangement you do not fully understand; therefore, an intelligent investment never involves being "sold" something you are unfamiliar with.

Placing your savings into an insurance product presented to you as a "sound investment," based solely on the advice of an insurance salesman or bank employee who solicited you, is a perfect example of something an intelligent investor should *never* do.

Neither is it an intelligent investment to purchase stocks based on the recommendation of a cold-calling broker because you believe he knows more than you do and has your interests at heart, *which is not likely*.

The correct term for those actions is naïveté, and that is a quick way to end up wearing patched pants and flip-flops.

An intelligent investor might speak with an agent to purchase a particular insurance product his financial advisor has determined ahead of time the investor needs, or he may be watching a particular opportunity unfold and call his stockbroker to make a purchase.

The investor may have put these matters into the hands of a full-time professional money manager, but he is too savvy to be "sold" a "great investment" by a stranger.

An intelligent investor puts convincing stories about completely safe high investment returns in the same category as children's fairy tales.

You may have heard of people foolishly "investing" years of savings after listening to a convincing sales pitch. It happened to a friend of mine. He was an electrician, and, after a lifetime full of hard work, he and his wife had managed to set aside $500,000. Wow! What discipline! Unfortunately, being disciplined, or even careful, is not the same as being savvy. Just before they were to retire, they lost it all to a good storyteller promising large profits with complete safety for their retirement years.

Having known him to be such a kind and hardworking person, I was deeply saddened even to hear about this. He is an honest, hard-working, trusting, fine man. Unfortunately, in the world of money, honest people can be at a great disadvantage because of their friendly and trusting nature. Hustlers and swindlers practice their craft and rely on the average person's unwillingness to refuse someone who seems friendly, helpful, informed, and courteous.

> A liar is always lavish of oaths.
> —Pierre Corneille

The world is full of designing people who will explain to you how you can get richer by giving *them* your money When a man with money but no experience meets a man with experience and no money, the man with the experience gets the money—and the man who used to have the money gets some "experience".

Remember this: the loss of capital—savings available for investing—is always more painful than the loss of opportunity. Remind yourself of that and then turn away from rose-colored investment stories.

Never do business with someone who solicits you first. Don't be sold!

Be Patient

> **2. Prudent investment beyond regular contributions requires the patient hoarding of cash for long periods of time until an attractive opportunity—one fully understood by *you* with no need for someone else to explain it—presents itself.**

We'll talk much more about this in the pages to come.

In a nutshell, an intelligent investor is far more concerned about the sudden loss of cash from a foolish blunder than about losing out on potential profits. An intelligent investor is comfortable walking away from any opportunity he or she does not understand. The relatively slow erosion of purchasing power by inflation is inconsequential when compared to the cost of a major investment mistake.

In a word, the intelligent investor is patient. When you wait for an investment that is out of favor with other buyers and has a place in your predetermined plan, and when you wait until you know that once you invest you can afford to hold your position . . . well, there isn't much risk. *That* is intelligent investing.

As you will soon see, this is not difficult to do. All one needs is a written plan, the sense to review it before acting, and the discipline to stick to those guidelines. In fact, that's Ground Rule #3.

Plan Ahead

3. Have an investment plan you are comfortable with.

The intelligent investor really must have a plan. My suggestions for an investment plan are not complicated. (By now, I'm sure that does not surprise you.) But that still does not mean my plan is the right one for everyone, and I do not make that claim.

Rather, I would say my thoughts should be helpful for those, like most of us, who are not financially sophisticated. My plan, or something like it, will protect your capital as well as can be done for the typical investor. If you follow something similar to it, you will never have to worry about the three most common reasons for a permanent loss of capital.

What are the three most common reasons for a permanent loss of the wealth you have available for investing? You may already know the answers to that question without realizing it.

Here are what I think are the three most common reasons for a serious loss of savings. See if you agree with me.

1. Doing something with a large portion of your money you are not experienced at—for example: trading stocks, buying an excessive amount of real estate relative to your experience level, or putting a big chunk of your money into some arrangement that is "guaranteed to double in value."

2. Giving a large portion of your money to someone who approached you with a convincing moneymaking idea. This would include "free" investment seminars being advertised in your town or some "expert" on television telling you what is about to triple in price.

Doing something with a small portion of your money, say ten percent or less, to improve yourself or your investment skills is very different from being gutted financially by a slick presentation.

3. Watching the entire stock market or real estate market or gold market collapse with all your money in that one thing.

As my investment advisor is also a close friend of mine, and he will certainly read this book, let me get some facts out in the open. After all, he knows the truth about my failures.

This knowledge evolved from my mistakes. To my embarrassment, I did every one of these costly things. So, I had to come up with some rules or go broke. Frustrated, I made a list of investments I understood. I decided that from that day forward I would limit my investing to those things I clearly understood and that I had written out in a predetermined plan.

As my irregular income did not allow for investing at regular paycheck intervals, I would now buy only when I was compelled to do so by the price being offered. It did not mean things couldn't get cheaper after I bought them, but it did put an end to me losing money faster than I could save it.

Before this change in approach, I would chase what was hot—too dumb to realize that if it was hot and featured on all the financial channels—the profits had already been made in the vast majority of cases.

I understood cash. Who doesn't? I understood the value of owning stocks and some gold and silver. And I had always made money on the homes I owned, so I decided real estate had to be a part of my plan. I knew I wanted the maturity that comes from learning the art of opportunistic investing. By that, I mean learning to improve on my judgment and take action only when acting was prudent. So, a small portion of my investment funds would be set aside for that as well.

Here is my plan for how I invest any money I accumulate now that I am out of debt and not nearly as foolish. The percentages are approximate.

1. Ten percent will be held in cash.
2. Ten percent will be held in gold and silver.
3. Thirty to forty percent will be invested in stocks.
4. Thirty to forty percent will be used to purchase and pay off rental real estate.
5. Ten percent will be held for special opportunities.

Now that you've been introduced to why I had to make some rules for myself and the basic outline of my plan, read on to learn why I chose those asset classes.

CHAPTER 4
THE PLAN: WHERE TO INVEST

*Do only what makes you most comfortable
when making money decisions.*

My plan for my own version of intelligent investment involves putting my savings in one of five different places. These five are assets that the average investor can typically understand and easily access, and they each deserve some attention of their own.

Remember: *Intelligent investing precludes participating in any financial arrangement you do not fully understand.*

Cash

One should always hold some of his or her wealth in cash. For one thing, it makes you a better investor to know you have a reserve of ready cash on hand. Also, in any economic or personal crisis, *cash is king.* Holding ready cash is like an experienced general keeping a reserve of fighting forces protected from frontline action, just in case.

Besides, a certain amount of cash is necessary. With cash you can make an investment, buy a loaf of bread, or go out to dinner. It is the essential medium of exchange. Resist the temptation to look down on holding some of your savings in idle cash.

There is a limit, however, to how much should be held in cash. That will vary from one person to the next, depending on the nature of their business, the reliability of their income, and their temperament.

Don't keep idle cash in large amounts, as it's not a safe place to store purchasing power long term due to inflation. A good guide is to hold enough of your total wealth in cash for you to be comfortable mentally about your situation and dispassionate about your investments.

Once you have that much set aside, you may then disregard the guideline of holding ten percent of your wealth in cash and instead, allocate any additional money saved among other assets. How much cash do I now hold? I keep enough cash set aside to run my household for six months.

I have an acquaintance—a lot smarter and wealthier than I—who stays fully invested. He said, if he ever gets into a tight place, he will sell something to raise the cash. That works for him, but I'm not comfortable with that. It just isn't me.

I recommend in every instance, no matter what someone else does, including me, you do only what makes you most comfortable when making money decisions.

Gold and Silver

Gold is real money. It has been for five thousand years and will be five thousand years from now. Governments can't print gold. Silver is real money, too, but perhaps a little less so. Not as highly esteemed as gold, it is still a precious metal with intrinsic value, and you should own some of it. I prefer a weighting of sixty or seventy percent gold and the balance in silver.

THE PLAN: WHERE TO INVEST

Since I am going to hold some of my excess capital in dollars, gold and silver will help to offset the effect of inflation on my cash. As dollars diminish in value, more of them will be necessary to buy the gold and silver I hold. As the nations of the world devalue their currency—almost in competitive fashion so they may more easily pay their national debts and gain an advantage with exports—the value of gold should rise as measured against the paper currencies of the world.

And gold and silver are highly liquid. This means that a good bit of my wealth is held in cash or in precious metals immediately convertible to cash—not a minor point in a crisis.

There are several ways to buy and hold gold and silver, and all of them are easy. One question is whether to hold the metal itself in the form of coins (bullion) or to hold the stocks of mining companies. Assuming you have access to a storage arrangement to keep the physical gold safe from theft, I would suggest a lay investor hold the metal itself, and as means increase, maybe a minor percentage in mining stocks.

Why do I prefer to own coins? My main reason is this: if you choose actually to take delivery of the metal and store it, you are less likely to sell a gold coin than you are a gold mining stock. Gold or silver coins represent real wealth, just as your home does, and you will not be as concerned about daily price quotes when you have the physical asset tucked safely away somewhere.

Once you have possession of the metal, it is yours. A mine can be flooded in an earthquake, or nationalized—a nice word for having it stolen by a cash-starved government—laborers can go on strike, or profits can be eroded by government regulations and rising taxation at the point of extraction.

I would not avoid mining stocks altogether, however, because occasionally they are so out of favor they are almost thrown away by the market. That can make them very cheap. Also, any profits from the sale of mining stocks are treated as normal capital gains for tax purposes, whereas the government discourages the population from holding the metal itself by taxing any profits made upon sale at a higher rate.

To buy coins, you have two choices:

1. Locate a dealer from a reliable referral.
2. Purchase bullion through a fund that takes your money and buys and stores the coins or bars for you.

Shares in the Central Fund of Canada (trading symbol: CEF) can be purchased through your stock brokerage firm. They will take your money and buy approximately sixty percent in gold bullion and forty percent in silver bullion and store it for you. The shares can be bought and sold at will, just like a stock. No muss; no fuss.

You can also purchase gold through a gold exchange-traded fund (for example, SPDR Gold Shares; trading symbol: GLD) and silver through a silver fund (for example, iShares Silver Trust; trading symbol: SLV). Though, from what I have been told of their prospectus, it is debatable whether they actually take the physical metal off the market and hold it for you as Central Fund of Canada does. It is probable they instead buy options to cover their positions.

When I am buying metals for a trade, I might use GLD or SLV or one of the other exchange-traded funds. When I am buying for a long-term hold, I use CEF. There are also other strictly silver or gold funds that do hold the metal itself for you. A broker with the ability to confirm that the holdings of the particular trust you are considering are audited would be helpful. Someone needs to be confirming annually that the metal they claim to have is actually in their possession. Your broker can advise you of the reliable precious metal funds operating in whatever year you are reading this book.

If you wish to buy shares in mining stocks, you can purchase one of several exchange-traded funds (for example,

VanEck Vectors Gold Miners ETF; trading symbol: GDX) that represent a cross-section of the mining companies.

I do not recommend you invest in new or speculative mining companies. Most exploratory mining or oil/gas drilling ventures are just a hole in the ground with a liar standing next to it. If anyone involved were truly certain they were going to hit big deposits . . . well, it is unlikely that the retail public could get a share if they offered their next three children.

As with any investment, make the purchase only when there is a bargain price being offered. Gold and silver prices are volatile, and patience will be rewarded. If I were looking to add to my positions in gold or silver, I would be looking to do so when either or both were out of favor. Because gold and silver prices are mercurial, buy them when they are unpopular, such as when the stock market is red-hot and the world is relatively calm, then just ride out the ups and downs. Trading in and out of a position purchased as a long-term hold is reserved for men and women who are a lot smarter than I am. Or a lot dumber.

Finally, traditional stock market investors disparage gold as a relic and point out that the overall stock market has outperformed gold for long periods at a time. This is true, but I am not pitting one against the other. My point is that gold is real money, and no government can print more of it.

Stocks

Most people understand what stocks are, and there are many different ways to buy them.

Picking individual stocks certainly increases risk. For the purposes intended here, let us assume you need only to select the exchange-traded funds or mutual funds of your choice. Or, again, if you have enough to qualify, you could instead open a professionally managed account.

Remember: a professional using a tactically managed approach to investing can take positions to profit in a rising or declining market, move to neutral positions, or adjust the percentage held in cash up and down with no tax consequences to you.

One caveat: a good pro will manage for safety first. Don't be looking to see how much money he or she is making you every month.

If you are acting on your own, I suggest you either invest in stock funds at regular intervals, such as when investing a set amount out of each paycheck, or only when stocks are out of favor.

Real Estate

As buying a rental property is costly, I wish to say a few words to the young saver. If you are young and struggling to save, buying a rental home will probably be out of reach for you. When I was younger I debated whether it was better to work toward having $200,000 saved and invested elsewhere, or own a paid for rental that netted me $1,000 a month (these are year 2020 price figures for homes in my area). As I aged I realized that, for me, the income was better than the liquid savings.

Now that I am older, all the money I can save to invest is earmarked for buying more rental income. If you can have a rental or two paid off by retirement age, that regular income is a lifelong comfort. It is difficult to save enough cash to live on for very long. But a rental can be paid for by the tenants and then provide you with life-long cash flow. Just one or two paid for rental homes are a fabulous boost to late-in-life planning.

Early on in life, if you cannot afford a rental home, and most can't, just start working toward saving the down-payment with whatever means your life-path provides to you. Keep it as a goal in your mind. It will never happen if you don't think about it, and it can happen in surprising ways if you keep

THE PLAN: WHERE TO INVEST

it in your mind. In the meantime, apply your savings to the parts of the plan you can do.

Now for a few general comments on the subject.

Debt used to create wealth presupposes a yield and therefore is proper *within manageable limits*. Real estate is a reliable investment made even more attractive by the way it is treated in the tax code and by the leverage—borrowed money—that can be safely used to acquire it.

In addition to the many books available on the subject, educational courses on real estate investing are offered around the country. These courses can be quite expensive, and I would recommend, that if you have an interest in real estate as a business as opposed to a passive investment vehicle, you pick one technique of real estate investing, pay for that one course of instruction only, and turn at least one profitable deal using that method before paying for additional instruction.

Trying to learn more than one technique at a time is expensive and can be counterproductive. Learning one method of real estate investing well enough to make consistent money is enough to undertake as a beginner.

Remember: investing in real estate as a business—a way to become self-employed—is an entirely different matter from my suggestion to invest a portion of your savings in real estate as an alternative to stocks.

Every book I have ever read on the subject teaches maximum leverage to control the greatest amount of property in order to create long-term wealth through appreciation. That is something to gradually grow into rather than leap into.

In your early forays into any new venture, my personal opinion is that you should avoid trying to juggle too many balls at one time. Prudent debt levels have easily manageable payment schedules; that is what makes them prudent. So do not get carried away and try to become a real estate mogul in a short period of time.

I know someone who bought ten highly leveraged properties for rentals during the last real estate boom. As I am writing, today the market has gone soft and he can't unload them or rent them for enough to get out from under the debt. He jumped into a hot market with both feet, and that's not how to acquire a new skill and stay solvent.

Personally, if I invest in rental real estate, I am seeking to place thirty percent of my free cash in an asset to receive a monthly income. Appreciation, if it ever occurs, is a bonus. When I use borrowed money to buy a rental property, my intention is to pay it off as quickly as possible.

Even if you decide to use more than thirty percent of your investment capital for real estate, keep your ten percent position in cash and your ten percent position in gold and silver. That is your fallback money.

> ***In any business, but especially in real estate, marginal players do not survive economic downturns.***

Buying a rental should not be a difficult decision, especially with the help of a real estate agent who is also a real estate investor.

Here are some of the questions I ask myself:

- If I needed a place to stay and I was a decent sort of guy, would I live here?
- Is this home in good condition or can I restore it to good condition and still get a return?
- Would my preferred type of tenant be comfortable moving into this home and neighborhood?
- Would I be comfortable and safe coming here to look after the property?
- Can I get an immediate positive cash flow?

THE PLAN: WHERE TO INVEST

- What will be my net return on rent income from the total spent when the deal is complete?

Real estate is a vast financial subject and one I am not qualified to write about. I bought mine the old-fashioned way. When I had the money and the opportunity, I put as much down as I could and then paid it off as quickly as possible.

If you decide to approach real estate as a business, with some research of your own you can find the method of real estate investing which appeals most to you: foreclosures, rehabbing and flipping, raw land, etc. If you develop a passion for it, the percentages of other asset classes could be adjusted to allow more room in your budget for this.

If tenants and maintenance seem too time-consuming for you, skip it, and use this money for one of the other asset classes, or just buy raw land in an area where growth is likely in the next decade. With professional counsel you could also choose to buy bonds or bond funds if the interest rates being paid appealed to you for cash flow.

Speculation

My fifth place in which to invest is speculation— what I call opportunistic investment. I want to learn to see opportunity and act upon it intelligently. I set aside ten percent of my investment funds for that purpose. However, if waiting for special opportunities does not appeal to you, then put that ten percent somewhere else.

Opportunistic investments should be reserved for situations that appear to have a real chance at a 100 percent advance in value. This is the easiest rule to violate and the most important rule to strictly follow.

I approach this decision in this way; I ask myself: "If this had to increase one hundred percent in price or I would lose *all* of my money invested here—would I still consider this completely safe?"

To risk funds held for special opportunities to gain only a marginal profit is pointless.

The majority of men and women who decide to become financially independent are going to become more alert to opportunities naturally. However, I can tell you from experience, if you hold ten percent for special opportunities, *don't spend time looking for something to do with it.* That will prove costly. There will be too many false temptations.

This cash is only for those rare occasions when something just jumps out at you and strikes you immediately with full clarity. Violating this rule of *not* actively looking for something to do with this passive cash will likely cost you. This is just money set aside for when there is a crisis of some kind and bargains are evident.

Cash . . . gold and silver . . . stocks . . . real estate . . . speculation. These are the five legs of my plan. Simply having a plan doesn't make you an intelligent investor, but it keeps you from being haphazard about investing, it helps you focus your thinking, and it is a good first step.

You need to stick to that plan.

CHAPTER 5
THE PLAN: STICKING TO IT

You're in control.

With my simple plan, I am as much in control of my invested capital as is attainable practically. The majority is always liquid. Leverage is minimal, only applying to any debt on the real estate.

Best of all, I will never have to hear my wife ask me, "What happened to all our money?"

Making It Easy

Not a lot of judgment is required to follow this plan. That's what makes it so easy to stick to.

First, cash is cash. That's easy.

Second, when I buy gold or silver coins, I intend to hold them. I'm not prescient enough to be a trader. If I bought them when the price declined and it continues to decline further, I won't complain. I will add to my position when I can. Gold is never going to become worthless or declare bankruptcy due to accounting fraud.

Third, stock funds are a great way to participate in the world's economic progress. If you buy stock funds for the long term, ignore the crises that come and go. Instead, look at that money the same way you look at your house when prices fluctuate: as something of value you are holding on to.

Fourth, comfortably owning a rental home or a piece of land only requires you to avoid making any purchase that exceeds your holding power.

Fifth, that last ten percent is used for any special opportunity that may come to my attention. It is the only portion I must decide when to take a loss or sell for a profit.

Who's in Control?

This plan eliminates a lot of the emotional and mental back-and-forth that so often accompanies investment decisions—and it eliminates a lot of risk. Of course, you can buy gold or a home at the wrong price and time—and I certainly have—but those things are hard assets with intrinsic value, and you will survive a misstep.

If you haven't overreached.

And with stocks, smart investors agree you either need to be investing regularly regardless of price or only buy during a fire sale. I can choose which of those two methods suits me best, and so can you. You're in control. Just know this is long-haul stuff and we all will be short-term wrong in our choices occasionally.

Notwithstanding the occasional mistake, I think this is doable for anyone. The real losses come from trying to pick the next highflier. Remember: when it comes to buying stocks, turn off the television. The men and women really making money are not telling anyone about it on TV, and the ones promoting stocks on television have private motives for their suggestions that may not include your prosperity.

THE PLAN: STICKING TO IT

When I am making investment decisions, I do often consult with my financial mentor. But, frankly, I have found repeatedly that no one knows what is going to happen tomorrow.

When considering an investment, I have found that, for me, my best defense is to reread what I have written in this book. In this way, I am able to double-check that I am not violating my own plan or rules. These few hours spent reading is about self-discipline and safety in following a plan. For me, this read-through serves as my safety check before I part with my money. I consider it cheap insurance.

Of course, if you are using a pro to handle your money, *that* is your plan—and it is a good one. But I still encourage regular conversations.

My plan is simple and certainly not unique to me. Men and women smarter than I am commonly recommend something similar, and it can be easily adjusted to suit your own preferences. And those preferences can change as you learn how better to manage your savings.

And one way we learn is by making mistakes. Mistakes cannot be completely avoided.

Even though losses are painful, they are inevitable, and there is no substitute for the wisdom that comes from making a few errors of your own. In fact, no matter what I or anyone else writes about money, you will make more than a few mistakes and those mistakes will teach you how to apply the rules you thought you already knew.

One more time: the best teachers you will ever have are your own mistakes.

> **Keep some cash in the bank for emergencies.**

Keep It Simple

For anyone who dreads the thought of making decisions with money, *just keep it simple*. Follow my plan to set aside some cash; then, as you can afford it, put a little into a gold and silver fund, preferably bought when prices are relatively low. Invest regularly in stocks no matter what is happening in the market. Or, just wait until there is a crash in stock prices; then load up and never look back.

Only if it suits your interests and lifestyle … buy a rental you can pay off within ten years or so.

I do, however, wish to reemphasize one earlier caution. The majority of books written about real estate investment recommend a course of low equity and high leverage to maximize the amount you own. This is fine if your objective is to create wealth through real estate and you have the necessary judgment and experience and income to handle the debt obligations wisely. Remember: in my financial plan, we are not discussing creating wealth in real estate, but using real estate as an alternative to the stock market for some of your savings.

If you don't want to be involved in investing at all, choose an autopilot program. Just keep some cash in the bank for emergencies, put ten percent of your money into a gold and silver fund, place the balance in stock funds at regular intervals, and ignore your monthly statements. If you ever have a windfall, buy a rental property or a piece of land.

Important: once you get within five years of retirement, you might want to begin transitioning to lower levels of stock holdings. There are mutual fund companies with funds set up to make automatic adjustments for age. The reasoning? You don't want to have all your money caught up in a market crash just before you begin relying on the account meant to help fund your retirement.

So . . . a couple of simple plans, both of which you control as much as such control is possible. But I want to say this loud and clear:

> *You can also skip all this and simply put some money into mutual funds and the bank and forget about doing anything else.*

THE PLAN: STICKING TO IT

If anything causes you worry or stress,
then don't do it*!*

Saved money should be a comforting, not a worrisome, thing, and it is important to keep that straight, whether the "experts" agree with our choices or not.

My plan is not suitable for everyone. If you are already a sophisticated investor, you don't need any advice from me. If, due to the nature of your work, you travel a lot or relocate often, then investing in rental property may be impractical for you.

Modify the plan to suit yourself but do consider keeping a portion of your funds in cash, gold, stocks, and maybe real estate or some other income-producing investment. And have some rules for when and how much you buy—i.e., what percentage of your money you will hold in each asset.

Honestly, sticking to my simple plan may not give me the highest return on my money, but it will almost certainly give me the return *of* my money—along with some profits from inflation.

The story goes that, once every thousand years, a black swan is born. For investors, a "black swan" refers to an external event that can't be anticipated. A shrewd investor will have a plan to survive the appearance of a black swan.

By sticking to my plan, I am ready if a black swan appears!

CHAPTER 6
THE PLAN: MANAGING IT

If you do not understand it ... if you cannot explain it to a sixth grader ... stay out of it.

The money you use to pay off debt can't be lost. But, once you begin to invest, your emphasis must be on risk control, not profit. Remember: the title of this book is *Invest Like a Wealth Manager*, and, as I noted in the introduction, wealth managers do their thinking and investing, first and foremost, to keep assets *safe*.

Managing your plan to protect your capital must become the first consideration in every decision. In this chapter, I will share with you how to do this.

> The essence of investment management is the management of risks, not the management of returns.
> —Benjamin Graham

Keep Mistakes Small

First, as we mentioned in the last chapter, in the investment of capital mistakes will be made. In fact, mistakes are helpful and necessary to acquire your own wisdom. **But follow a sound set of rules to keep the mistakes small.**

THE PLAN: MANAGING IT

Even if you never intend to make your own investment decisions, this book's discussion of managing your assets, including acting on special opportunities, can make you more grounded and deliberate with money.

Below are my own six rules, learned the hard way, to keep the size of the inevitable investment mistakes manageable. Most people, of course, will make their investments at regular intervals out of their paychecks into investment funds of their choice. That makes these rules most applicable for monies held for exceptional opportunities, though they may apply to any investment you make. I really think the list is valuable to have for review no matter how you invest.

1. Never make an investment simply because you have become impatient holding cash. NEVER.

2. Never allow yourself to be tempted to treat that which is only probable as if it were certain.

3. Investing in an individual stock that hold great potential is still speculative, so it should either be done with the ten percent you have set aside in your plan for special opportunities, or you may want to limit that kind of investment to a rational percent of the total funds you have allocated for stocks. Either way, your exposure should not be so great in an individual stock that years of effort can be wiped out.

   By holding back a good amount of your money—the right thing to do whenever you invest in anything that involves risk factors you cannot personally control—you are insuring yourself against large mistakes. Of course, on occasion, that means you will not make as much, but that is the price of insuring yourself against unrecoverable losses.

When you know that most of your money is unexposed to the ups or downs of one event, it allows you to be patient and detached as you give the investment time to develop. If you are emotionally uninvolved, you will also be more willing to admit a mistake and take a loss when it is clearly prudent to do so.

If, in order to increase potential profits, you raise the stakes to levels that can hurt you if the investment turns against you, then you are no longer participating in intelligent investing. You are gambling.

4. I have seen investments that marketed as sound and safe, which required signing off on multiple pages of inscrutable fine print. If you do not understand it . . . if you cannot explain it to a sixth-grader . . . *stay out of it!*

5. If you invest in real estate, be sure you can cover the payment for a while. Don't be dependent on renting immediately to cover your expenses. Have enough money somewhere to cover the note yourself for six months in the event you lose your tenant or cannot acquire a desirable tenant quickly.

   An eviction can be expensive and take a long time, and the possibility of such unpleasantness can be greatly reduced if you can afford to hold out for the right tenant.

   Often it takes longer than you expect to get a quality occupant, and you don't want to be in the position that you have to rent to the first person who comes along. That just guarantees bigger problems later.

   I allowed the rental home I own to remain vacant for over a year while I held out for the tenant I wanted.

THE PLAN: MANAGING IT

It was worth it. She keeps the home immaculate and always pays the rent on time. I didn't like waiting, but I could afford to because I had built a financial margin into my purchase decision.

6. Don't overreach. Never make an investment that would take you down with it if it went wrong. As I heard someone say once: "Never risk your home for a chance at a palace."

Following these rules will keep your mistakes manageable.

Being in Control

Intelligent investing means that we have a plan for consistent and clear control.

If you invest at regular intervals and do not stop when values decline, the discipline to do that *is* your long-term control.

If you use a professional, that pro is your control. Still, stay in touch with him or her once a quarter. It is human nature to give more attention to accounts that are engaged with the manager.

If you have a simple allocation plan for how much and what kind of assets you buy, and you follow those percentages, and especially if you buy the assets when they are out of favor, then your patience to invest against the trend is your control, your safety net.

Any of these methods that you prefer for your current circumstances at the time, diligently adhered to, will work for you in the long term.

Here is what will *not* work: chasing hot stock tips from television and magazines or listening to promoters who solicit you. Even if you happen to get lucky with an individual stock, that will only encourage you in a dangerous practice.

Assets you choose to buy at regular intervals out of your paycheck—such as 401(k) contributions to retirement programs—do not require patience. But when it comes to discretionary purchases the patience to wait on a real opportunity—usually some type of price collapse in that asset—is critical.

Impatient money is at risk.

Why am I stressing the point that one should wait for a clear bargain? Because in my opinion, markets are no longer controlled by values and logic.

Computer trading . . . interest-rate manipulation by central banks . . . money masters moving markets behind the scenes . . . and other factors which cannot be anticipated or understood . . . are the new powers. Not logic or values.

Movers of money create a stampede out of some asset class and then move in and pick up the bargains they themselves created. For the proactive investor, the correct time to act is after we see which way the wind blows, so to speak. To make a big speculative investment based on what we think *should* happen is like trying to buy diamonds by moonlight.

When making an opportunistic investment I have profited long term when I bought after a sell-off—and invariably lost when I bought on some supposition of my own about what should happen in the near future.

And there is a double penalty with this mistake. You lose the money when you are wrong, either selling for a loss or waiting for years for the price to recover, and you have decreased your ability to make a profitable investment when a real one shows up.

Imagine an American football game in which the game is tied, and a team is on the opponent's one-yard line, about to score the go-ahead touchdown. Instead, they fumble the ball and the opposing team runs it all the way back to the other end of the field and ends up scoring seven points—six for the touchdown and one more for the extra point kick. That is not a seven-point swing; that is a *fourteen*-point swing the wrong way, in one play.

Making exactly that mistake with half my money is what it took to teach me to follow my own rules for safety without exception. And especially if you choose to make an opportunistic investment you must wait until there is an indisputably clear situation before you, not when you rationalize that a certain scenario might occur. What exactly do I mean by indisputably clear? In my lifetime, on average about once every five to eight years, I have seen something of value—stocks, gold, or real estate—collapse in price by forty percent or more. That is what I mean. I have also seen many times when everything was expensive.

After my last misjudgment, I told my wife, "The next time I tell you that I am putting our money into something, I want you to tell me to show you the fire. If a crisis creating a fire-sale opportunity hasn't been headlining the financial news for the last few months, *tell me to put our checkbook away.*"

Keep in mind, the slow erosion of your money from inflation is inconsequential compared to a serious loss of capital from an impatient blunder. This is the most reliable lesson I have learned from my mistakes: **the profits are made when you buy, not when you sell**.

One correct investment decision is more than enough to offset many years of decline in purchasing power due to inflation.

The mark of an intelligent investor is the ability to sit patiently with idle speculative funds—for five to eight years if necessary—until an opportunity appears with which they are completely comfortable.

Beyond regular stock contributions to a retirement account, regarding occasional discretionary investments, a mature investor keeps his or her eyes open—better yet, only half-open—and feels no need to be "doing something" or to "have my money working." This has been a costly lesson for me. I finally learned it, but at great expense.

Getting out of debt—which *is* investing for your future—is the only time you will never be at risk of making an error.

True, I have had large losses relative to our means, but they have never affected our family because I had gotten out of debt first and, by the grace of God, did not need the money.

CHAPTER 7
THE PLAN: SPECULATION

*No one has to invest speculatively.
Only do so if it interests you.*

I hope I have stressed enough that there are simple, smart things we each can do with our money. That's what the plan is all about. These include keeping a percentage in cash . . . buying gold and silver . . . investing at regular intervals in stocks through exchange-traded or mutual funds . . . buying a rental home that will produce a positive cash flow or investing in raw land with the potential for population growth coming toward it. With professional guidance one may even participate in the more advanced products described in Appendix 2. Once we have sufficient assets to qualify we can consider using a professional to manage our investments in a tactical manner, responding to market changes quickly.

All are good things to do with money—long term. But what about when all the prudent steps are covered financially, and something just appeals to you? What about when you think you are looking at an opportunity to make some real money? Our plan should allow for such speculations as they are often clearly safe and profitable when they occur.

A Simple Test for Speculative Investment Decisions

Remember: no one has to invest speculatively. Only do so if it interests you. If waiting for this kind of opportunity does not appeal to you, then use the 10 percent I set aside for this to some other part of your plan.

Personally, I want to learn to see opportunity and act upon it intelligently. So, in the years that I can, I do hold some percent of my investment funds for this purpose.

This does not mean however, that I jump into everything that comes along. Instead, I start with a simple test, asking myself these questions whenever I consider such an investment:

- Is it practical?
- Is it probable?
- Is this suitable for me, considering where I am right now financially?
- Can I handle it if this turns against me? Can I cope with a worst-case scenario?

A negative answer to any of these questions means *Keep Out!*

I like to remember a quote by the late Hetty Green. Hetty, born in 1834, was eventually worth over $100 million in a day and time when most women rarely left their homes. I read somewhere that at one time she held the mortgages on some of the most valuable real estate in New York. Hetty was a true miser and certainly not someone I admire, but she put the subject of intelligent investing into two sentences:

There is no secret in fortune-making.
All you have to do is buy cheap and sell dear,
act with thrift, and shrewdness, and be persistent.

THE PLAN: SPECULATION

To put that into even plainer language: don't act like the crowd. Buy it from them when nobody wants it and sell it back to them when everybody wants it again.

So, if an intelligent investor is interested in buying real estate, he waits to buy until he has a deal that makes sense at the closing table. If she is buying precious metals, she waits until the stock market is hot and no one has any interest in anything else—and the price of precious metals reflects this.

If he is buying stocks, he does so at regular intervals, ignoring ups and downs, or buys after the market has taken some big hits and refuses to decline further on more bad news. Why does he do this? Because with either method, the investor is safe *long-term*.

Of course, opportunities *can* come to us in ways other than a market decline. An acquaintance of mine had some friends start up a local bank and they let him in on the deal for early shares. He sold later for one million dollars profit.

But the point is, a savvy investor is not trying to jump onto moving trains out of fear of being left behind. Experienced investors will not compromise the long-term safety of their investment capital chasing a pot of gold.

This will mean long periods of time when a mature investor is quite content to do nothing at all but save cash while waiting for a clear and compelling opportunity. I have learned to wait *until the buy price alone brings me complete satisfaction with my decision.* So, if the buy is not made so much because it has been "reasoned through" as a smart move, but rather because it is so clearly an exceptional opportunity that **the purchase price alone justifies what I am doing—and the purchase price alone actually satisfies me**—I should be long-term safe. And very likely, profitable.

What You Need to Be Able to Do

If you are inclined to venture into some speculative investment, then here is what you need to be able to do.

- As you are paying off your consumer debts (always the first step in managing your money—see *Riches Beyond the Bling*, the first book in this series), put together a simple plan for investing your soon-to-be-available capital.

- Follow that plan.

- Accumulate cash without feeling compelled to "do something" with it, holding your special opportunity money idle for years if necessary.

- Don't trust hot tips from television financial channels or rosy pitches delivered by professional promoters passing through town. Close your ears—and mind—to promises and pledges from people you don't really know about investments you don't really understand.

- Wait until an indisputable opportunity is lying on the ground in front of you, whether it be a sharp decline in gold prices, a crash in the stock market, or an attractively priced piece of land or rental home.

- *Then* make your investment.

If you can do these things, you will come out far ahead of the "investor" who is always trying to "make something happen." In hindsight, you may see where you have missed a few opportunities, but you will come out just fine in the long run.

Here's a good example of what I am talking about. I missed this opportunity by just a few days. A bank recently sold a house in a new subdivision down the road from my home in a

THE PLAN: SPECULATION

short sale—that means the bank will sell for less than is owed it on the loan—for thirty percent under construction costs.

Had I found that deal in time, no one could have convinced me I was making a mistake buying that home. *It was the buy price alone that justified the transaction, not some hopeful future scenario for a higher resell.*

In another opportunity some years back, silver was selling for less than nine dollars an ounce after having been over twenty dollars an ounce. Just seven months later, it was up more than seventy percent from its low. After you buy, you don't need a crystal ball to know when to sell in a case like this, assuming it was purchased for a profitable trade rather than a long-term hold. When you make fifty percent plus in half a year, just sell if prices start to turn south.

When it comes to speculative investments like this one, I try to keep in mind the advice for selling given by Joseph Kennedy, the wealthy father of President John Kennedy: "Only a fool holds out for the top dollar."

Of course, these opportunities are rare. The infrequent occurrence of such bargains is why you should not be trying to force your money to make profits for you when no opportunity is present. That only leads to death by a thousand cuts. Based on my experience, deals like this occur on average once every three to eight years, which is why you and I should use those years to accumulate some cash.

Years ago, I was listening to an interview with the billionaire investor Warren Buffett. He was asked why he held so much of his working capital in cash. He quipped, "When you hunt fast-moving game, you have to keep your guns loaded."

That is why I hold that ten percent of my investment funds in a "special opportunity account," and why I don't "dabble" with that portion of my money while I am waiting.

Learning Patience

I have had to learn patience the hard way, and that's true for most everyone. It is a lesson only truly acquired after a couple of our own impetuous mistakes. *Just because you have the money does not mean a buying opportunity is there at the same time.*

As I'm writing, gold is pricey. If I wanted to start or add to my own position in gold, I would not be buying now. However, real estate prices are very depressed, and I do need to add to my real estate position to achieve the proportionate weighting of approximately thirty percent of my invested capital held in that asset class. So, when I have gathered up my next bit of investment money, I will seek to use it there, if it is still on sale.

Of course, I will do nothing unless I find something I have a workable price on. After all, it is not the value of the real estate that determines the weight of your position, but your equity in it. I know that at the time this is being written, which is during a real estate depression, prices in real estate are low and probably will be for a long time, but instead of looking for something that can rise in price more quickly, I try to follow the advice attributed to financier and philanthropist Bernard Baruch: "Buy straw hats in the winter."

Accumulating cash while you patiently await a special opportunity right for you will take maturity—maturity evidenced by long periods of inactivity.

> *How will you know if the opportunity is right for you?*
> *If it is the right one for you, you will recognize it*
> *when you see it. That's how you know.*

Now, I am not recommending one wait a long time merely for the sake of waiting. Opportunities can come at any time.

I am suggesting we wait however long is required for a buying opportunity so clearly compelling that it just jumps

THE PLAN: SPECULATION

out at you. Until you recognize such an opportunity, follow this bit of advice from the late Will Rogers, commonsense American humorist: "The quickest way to double your money is to fold it and put it back in your pocket."

I have failed that "wait till the opportunity is clear" rule more than once. Probably so will you. But my words should cut the learning curve for you considerably. Truthfully, until we make our own mistakes, the rules intended to help us avoid them are just words on paper we only think we understand. Until you make an error and have the mistake cost you something, it is difficult to truly own the knowledge as a personal possession.

It is much like the young child who was warned not to touch the stove because it was hot, but having never been burned, found the concept too vague to understand, even though the instruction itself—don't touch—was simple and perfectly clear. However, after violating the rule once, the baby *knows* hot for himself—*and baby don't need a second time!*

Investing only when you have full understanding is not hard to do, even for the unsophisticated. Life will offer these opportunities to those patiently awaiting them. For example, a relative who will sell you a desirable piece of land for twenty percent less than market value is an example of a good deal that can be clearly understood. Though such unmistakable investment opportunities are usually years apart, they do occur and will continue to throughout your life.

Examples

I had clear investment opportunities occur in **1990**, **1993**, **1998**, **2003**, and **2008**, and I want to tell you about them now. These particular years, though perhaps distant past

> Even to make large amounts of money, I will not do anything that is a risk to capital. Twelve purchases made my career. A man would do well to limit himself to twenty in a lifetime.
> —Warren Buffett

to some of you readers, illustrate the types of events that will continue to happen throughout your own lifetime. Surely many other opportunities occurred during those years, but for most of that time I was not yet out of debt, and so was not attentive to such events.

These few however, were clear enough to just jump out at me, which is exactly the kind of opportunity you will be looking for—ones that simply make sense to you immediately.

In fact, I have found that the best way to accurately identify such opportunities is *not to look*. Instead, I just go about my life until something grabs my attention on its own. Trust me: when the price of some broadly held asset like homes or gold or stocks has fallen off a cliff, it *will* be in the news. And, when a more isolated opportunity occurs in your proximity—one appropriate for you—you will notice it.

For the instructive value specific examples can provide, we will now look at a few opportunistic investments that were clear to me: opportunities to buy real estate, an individual stock, stocks in general, and precious metals.

Example: 1990

In 1990 my wife and I spent our honeymoon at a surprisingly undiscovered beach town in the panhandle of Florida. The shore was pristine, with sand the texture of sugar and almost as white. We could sunbathe on the beach in the middle of summer and count on two hands the number of people in sight for a mile in either direction. The shell of an old building abandoned since the 1950s was sitting on some of the best oceanfront real estate I had ever seen.

I *knew* what this land was going to be worth in a few years. Unfortunately, at the time we had no money to invest. You didn't have to be rich enough to buy oceanfront property, anyone who could afford to purchase a lot or a little land in the area, and hold it, would be sure to reap large rewards. Today, you can't buy a postcard with a picture of the place on it for less than $100,000. So, we had to miss that chance, but nevertheless, this is a perfect example of a simple and safe opportunistic investment.

Example: Around 1993

In the early 1990s, a new start-up company went public. America Online (AOL) was on the cutting edge of the new craze for internet access and was being sold as the best way for people unfamiliar with computers to get online. The stock price had a long way to run whether the company made money or not.

Which it actually didn't. But creative accounting kept that fact hidden from investors while the stock price soared more than twentyfold within just twenty-four months of going public. Eventually AOL would have to write down $325 million in hidden losses—and investors still climbed into the stock! That's Wall Street for you.

Nevertheless, there was plenty of room to ride the first wave up, and hopefully, have enough sense to sell when the tumble down began in earnest. For me, this wasn't a hunch. A blind man could have seen this one. Especially when, in or around 1993, they had to stop taking subscribers for a time because they had outgrown their capacity. I *knew* I was looking at a great investment opportunity. And I didn't need anyone to explain it to me.

Unfortunately, I didn't buy a single share. Since we were furnishing our home at the time, I felt I needed to keep every dollar I could get my hands on. I passed on the opportunity because I wanted to complete that home furnishing project as quickly as possible without borrowing any money to do it. What a missed opportunity!

This was clearly a case of being too conservative, and it cost me. Had I invested just $5,000 of the money I was spending on furniture at the time, within a couple of years that investment would have paid me back all the money I spent furnishing the entire home.

Immediate Inconvenience

I learned a great lesson here. Opportunity comes when it comes. And it doesn't care if it is a convenient time for us. In fact, reaching back in my thoughts right now, I can't remember a single opportunity that came at a convenient time for me.

Instead, you will find that opportunity will test you right from the start by making an appearance when you are at your busiest, just to see if you respect its reward enough to stop everything else and embrace it. If you simply can't take advantage because you don't have the money, there is nothing you can do about that. But, if you have the means, you had better move decisively when a genuine opportunity presents itself, even if you have to put other important business on hold.

Our lives are filled with tight schedules, family obligations, prior commitments, problems at work—and all seem important at the time. But once every great while opportunity reaches her hand out to us amidst the press of these things. You will have to choose, and I urge you to act for the long term.

The best words to describe opportunity accurately are *immediate inconvenience*. Opportunity is almost always an immediate inconvenience. But opportunity will delay her offer for no one. She must be grasped in the moment she chooses and in no other. Half the risk management of life is not some act of caution, but the willingness to act decisively and to the exclusion of other business when a clear opportunity presents itself. Opportunities to make money are never lost, they are just taken by others who were wise enough to put everything else on hold.

THE PLAN: SPECULATION

For shrewd investors acting on an opportunity has three simple elements:

1. Do not act when there is no clear and immediately compelling opportunity. If you have to go back and forth mentally in doubt and debate, it is not clear enough. Real opportunities leap onto your sight and leave no room for debate.
2. Act immediately when a clear opportunity presents itself.
3. Act to the exclusion of other pressing business.

Example: 1998

That year, I had a chance to buy some prime land with a great view of the beautiful hills of north Georgia for $5,000 an acre. The owner had his home and the adjacent land listed for sale in the local newspaper and I went to take a look at it. As soon as I stepped out of the car I was overwhelmed by the views—and the obvious future value of the property. There was no hesitation this time. I took it.

Ten years later, my now paid-for home with surrounding land is worth well over one million dollars.

Example: 2003

This time the opportunity offered to the patient investor was the chance to buy stocks in general. In 2000, after one of the longest bull runs in market history, the world's stock markets, now highly overvalued, imploded.

In 2001, the market took another hit when terrorists attacked the United States. A war in Afghanistan ensued, and there was great uncertainty about whether US armed forces would also be ordered to invade neighboring Iraq.

You could feel the tension in the investment markets, and the world in general, like the edge of a knife. The stock market had been knocked down twice, and prices were on the mats. As soon as the war in Iraq began in 2003, the uncertainty was over. For better or worse, at least the world finally knew what direction things were taking.

All classes of stocks began to march higher, as if a huge weight had been lifted off the world's stock markets. Had I some money to invest at the time, it would have been an easy call to put some into stock funds. The harder call, as always, is when to sell, though selling need not be the intention. This was a great opportunity to enter the stock market for the long-term.

Don't Get Greedy

I have a friend who told me his method for selling an individual stock was no more complicated than this: "If something about the stock's price action makes the back of my neck tingle—*I sell*." I rather like his rule, if the intention when you bought it was to sell for a profit rather than hold long-term.

In any opportunistic investment, resist becoming greedy. At some point you *must* sell to capture your profits, or you will lose them. Do not be lulled into thinking of your speculative investment's monthly value statement as just numbers on a sheet of paper. They represent real dollars and real damage is done if they start to decline in earnest.

So once you have made a serious profit—say, fifty percent or more—you should never even let it get close to not being a profitable trade. Or worse yet, wait to sell until you have lost all profits plus some of your original investment.

Bernard Baruch, the famous stock speculator of the late 1800s, said that, many times, he sold a stock and then watched it double or triple from there. However, he did not concern himself with that at all. The object, he said, was to make—*then*

THE PLAN: SPECULATION

take—profits. He is said once to have remarked, "I always sell too soon. That is why I still have my fortune." In other words, you can only exit a stock safely when it has not reached its peak. It has to be done on the way up.

Of course, this would not apply if you invested with the intent of holding for the long term. Baruch was a speculator. Speculation does not mean sophisticated risk-taking. It means that, rather than invest and hold through the ups and downs, one waits until a particular opportunity is "observed" and reacts to it, either to purchase and hold for the long term or to sell later for a profit. Speculation comes from the same Latin root word that "spectator" comes from, and it means "to observe."

There need be no greater risk in opportunistic investment than in regular interval investing. Indeed, one might make the claim that there is less.

How can that be true?

When you invest automatically at regular intervals, you simply put your money in, and it never comes out of harm's way. You are in for the long haul; that's your strategy. And although that strategy is long-term safe, it has sustained some big declines in value in the last twenty years; declines that took the investors many years to recover from.

Seen in that way, putting money in and leaving it alone could be riskier than having a fairly competent speculative investor taking isolated opportunities for making a profit and then getting the money out before something bad happens.

I've heard good arguments for both sides, but I still think that for the great majority of us average people—and I definitely include myself in that category—regular interval investing is better suited to paychecks and human temperament because it puts the money to long-term use before we can be tempted to spend it. Safest of all is allowing a professional wealth manager to make the calls, but as we've talked about before, many of us never get to the point of having enough money for a professional to handle.

Bottom line: for the average worker, putting money into stocks through regular interval investing and leaving it alone is probably safer. But this is not a one or the other choice. For those that have the means and interest, doing both makes sense. Save and accumulate a small portion of your investment funds for those infrequent special opportunities if it appeals to you.

Example: 2008

In 2008, the largest banks and brokerage firms in the world became caught up in their own overleveraged webs as mortgage defaults in the subprime housing market spiraled out of control and triggered domino-effect losses. Suddenly, every bank, brokerage firm, and hedge fund needed cash to survive. Anything and everything with value was sold to raise capital. Gold, silver, and stocks were sold at any price in a frenzy to raise cash. Real estate prices went into a death spiral.

In a rare, coordinated effort, the central banks and governments of the world, led by the United States, collectively announced that trillions of dollars would be printed or borrowed to prevent the financial crisis from cascading into a global economic meltdown.

I knew this inflation—a sharp increase in the number of dollars printed and put into circulation—would cause a long-term decline in the value of all currencies. This decline in currency value should have a positive impact on the price of the gold and silver then being dumped to raise short-term capital. Simply put, it would take more of the devalued dollars to buy hard assets later.

I decided that if gold and silver continued to be thrown overboard to raise cash, I would buy silver at something near fifty percent off its previous high and hold it. Silver appealed to me as a trade more than gold since the swings in price are greater.

THE PLAN: SPECULATION

I borrowed $50,000 from my line of credit on a three-year, five percent, interest-only note, and, when the desired price came, bought four thousand ounces of silver. Of course, in a case like this, you never know how low something may go. You just have to decide at what price you feel you have a bargain and then live with it.

I also put in an order to make an additional $50,000 purchase if the price fell another thirty percent below my first buy point. I missed the second buy point by only twenty-one cents—*ouch*.

I had a three-year cost of capital of $7,500 in interest on the first $50,000 loan. If in three years the price of an ounce of silver increased only two dollars from my purchase price, I could exit even.

An additional consideration was that, unlike a stock, silver has intrinsic value. So there was no chance some unanticipated news of dishonest accounting or fraud would suddenly make my purchase worth less— or even worthless.

Considering the possible outcomes, I decided there was little downside risk. If the economy improved and inflation kicked in, I could make multiples of my cost of capital, and, with a little time, an eventual profit of 100 percent of the principal seemed reasonable.

If after three years the price appreciation I anticipated did not develop, I would simply pay the loan off and hold the silver, as I had many times that amount of cash in reserve. Therefore, *I had holding power.*

How did this work out for me? Well, I ended up selling for a forty percent profit. Had I decided to hold longer, the profit would have been 300 percent. I sold because I had something else I wanted to do with the money that was more important to me at the time. I was in control every step of the way.

An Expanded Checklist

Remember the "simple test" for judging investments of opportunity at the very beginning of this chapter? I think we're ready now for a more complete checklist. Use this list as a safety review before making such decisions.

1. Is it practical?
2. Is it probable?
3. Is this suitable for me, considering where I am financially?
4. Can I handle it if it turns against me? Can I handle a worst-case scenario?
5. Have I treated probability like certainty by making a disproportionately large investment?
6. Do I have holding power? If I am wrong in the short term, and the price continues to decline for a while, can I wait it out?
7. Does the purchase price alone justify my action?
8. Did someone else give this idea or is it my own judgment?

A review of the above questions will prevent you from getting irrational and acting like, as Warren Buffett has called them, a typical "know-nothing" investor.

When I made the leveraged investment in silver in 2008, I satisfied myself first with this series of questions, then submitted the same checklist to my wife for her input. All it would take was a single negative to call a halt and reevaluate. We found none.

Therefore, in my judgment, all the requirements for an intelligent speculative investment were present and I acted.

THE PLAN: SPECULATION

You might want to mark this page and when the time comes for you to consider an opportunistic investment, review this checklist. If you do, these questions alone will be worth a great deal more to you than whatever you paid for my five books.

Your Questions

It all seems so simple, doesn't it? But I know you still may have questions. Let's look at a couple of them.

If everything looked so good, why didn't you buy more and go for a bigger payoff?

Several reasons. For one thing, this was a speculative purchase for a trade. I already had my long-term position in gold.

I also did not want to treat that which was only probable and logical as if it were a certainty. In other words, I followed my own rules. Once you determine an opportunity is present, you must stick to prudent rules for how much to invest.

If I were investing in an individual stock, I would not risk more than ten percent of my total investment capital. (Another lesson learned the hard way.) If investing in an opportunity presented by a depressed price in gold or silver, I might go a touch higher as some sudden exposure of corporate misconduct or a poor earnings report could not enter the equation. And if I wanted to buy another rental property, I would use conservative projections for rental rates and occupancy and have enough money after the purchase to cover the note myself for six months if it became necessary. That way, I could wait for a desirable tenant.

The possibility of unanticipated events is an ever-present reality in life. Wise investment decisions always leave you some breathing room.

Here's another reason why I did not buy more and go for a bigger payoff. **Every investment requires holding power and time to succeed.** This is probably the most important reason you should keep a reserve of funds large enough to keep you comfortably neutral while your investment is given time to work.

**Before you put your money at risk,
be sure you have the ability to hold
because you will never control the time element.**

Remember, if you increase the size of the investment in order to increase the profits, you have switched from investing to gambling. As Ben Franklin wrote, "Great estates may venture more, but little boats should keep near shore."

What if I have set a three-year goal to have $50,000 invested, and, after saving the first $10,000, see an opportunity to make an investment in one of my chosen asset classes at a good entry price? Can I use all the $10,000?

Yes. In this case, the $10,000 is twenty percent of your current goal, and, if an opportunity to take a bargain in one of the classes of assets on your list comes up, you have to take it. And the $10,000 is for just that purpose.

Wait and Be Contrary

Though I was either not wise enough or not capitalized well enough to take advantage of most of the investment opportunities I have shared with you, they were all obvious to me at the time they occurred. Surely there were others during these years that I was not alert or sophisticated enough to see—opportunities that would have allowed a normal wage earner to put his or her savings to work at safer than normal prices.

You may not consider the investments I have mentioned particularly insightful, depending on your own level of financial sophistication. My only point in sharing them is to help you see that a sufficient number of investment opportunities that are suitable for us will occur in the course of our lives—and

THE PLAN: SPECULATION

it is important that **we wait** on them **and act contrary to the fears of the public** at the time.

Putting money into an "investment" simply because you have some free cash at the moment should be strictly avoided. (Again, this conversation does not apply to money invested at regular intervals out of your paycheck, but only to that portion of your cash reserved for special opportunities.)

My largest losses have come from becoming impatient after a few years of doing nothing, and then talking myself into making an investment when no legitimate investment opportunity existed. "Doing nothing" is actually the most profitable thing to do, and to continue to do, when doing nothing is what is called for.

As I said earlier in the chapter, constantly trying to make something happen results in death by a thousand cuts and investing your special opportunity savings before you are compelled to do so will result in painful losses and lessons. Special opportunity investing is not a constant activity, nor need it be a "big deal" or complex to be profitable.

The more years you save, the more you will have to profit from the next crisis. And that is the attitude to have until something of long-term value that has been greatly discounted appears. That can be hard to do when the economy is strong and market quotations are marching higher and you are sitting on a little money. In those times, keep reminding yourself that special opportunity funds are not your regular investment funds.

Instead, wait for those occasions when an individual stock or stocks in general, or gold and silver, or real estate, are quite inexpensive and out of favor. Popular sentiment will be that the asset should be avoided. That's when your waiting pays off and you invest contrary to the popular sentiment.

Bottom Line

The asset allocation percentages for general investing I have suggested will give most of us all the diversity we need, unless and until we are sophisticated enough to begin concentrating our investment dollars into a particular line of endeavor. If you want to invest more in stocks, or in anything else, you can always trim back the percentage you hold in some other asset class to make room for it.

Meanwhile, the majority of your wealth is easily convertible back into cash in the event of emergency, and if it suits your temperament, a percentage of your savings is reserved for those opportunistic investments that have a legitimate chance at a 100 percent advance in price.

But only go there if you enjoy that sort of thing. And be sure not to start out beyond the recommended ten percent for speculation. That is enough money to "go to school" with until you know what you are about with a spare dollar.

The rest is invested at regular intervals or into accounts managed by a professional. Yes, gold and silver will fluctuate widely in price (which is why you should buy only on a significant pullback in price), and the cash you hold will be eroded by inflation. But you should always keep a little free cash in reserve. Cash gives you peace of mind and makes you a better investor. And if that truly exceptional opportunity—or a crisis—arises, cash is a ready servant.

While I was writing this section of the book, my two younger daughters, Saige and Sierra, stopped at my desk and asked what I was writing about. After I had done my best to explain it to them, I playfully asked what they thought of my logic. Saige quipped, "If anyone holding all that stuff gets wiped out, *God's back*!"

CHAPTER 8
MORE HARD-WON TIPS

Never invest your money with anyone who approaches you first.

I've been told by at least one reader of early versions of my books that they benefitted from my writing style of repeating important points. I was gratified to hear that. I make points repetitively because they are the very points people overlook when investing. I made these very mistakes. In fact, I probably should've titled this book *A List of All the Stupid Things I Did in My Life with Money*.

The title, though, is *Invest Like a Wealth Manager*, and I believe the hard-won insights that make up this book, and especially this chapter, can help you do just that—think like a professional detached manager of your own wealth. Remember, as I said in the introduction,

> Wealth managers are the folks who allocate dollars across all major asset classes (for example, stocks, bonds, commodities, real estate, etc.), and they are trained mentally to act contrary to the herd to

do so. Their thinking and investing are done first and foremost to keep assets *safe*.

Read on for more advice on how to keep your assets safe.

Small Deals Can Make Money Safely

I have a friend who bought a few small townhome rental units and also did some big land investment deals. Years later, after he sold out, he told me that the small deals had made him five times his investment, in addition to all the years of income they provided. The big deals, however, that had tied up a lot of money and kept him worried, were barely break-evens.

I spoke with another Atlanta man who had an instructive story about smaller investments yielding large returns. When he was attending college, the building materials company The Home Depot was just starting up. He noticed how well the store was run and how people were crowding in. He put some of his college tuition money into the stock. In fact, he decided he would use the tuition money his parents had set aside to help him with college expenses to invest in the new company and borrow the money for tuition himself. When we spoke, he reported those few thousand he had invested decades ago were now $400,000 worth of stock.

I am not suggesting you try to catch lightning in a bottle. I *am* making a rational point to encourage us all: small, easy-to-put-together, easy-to-see deals and events, *can* make money. And they can give the average man or woman safe returns with less risk than the "big" deals people often hear of.

You and I don't need hundreds of thousands of dollars to invest. Five to ten thousand can be a lot when you wait until the moment is right.

MORE HARD-WON TIPS

The Most Common Cause of the "Big Loss"

Here is a cardinal rule for protecting your investment capital—one that will save you ten times more money than it will cost you over the course of your life:

> **Never invest your money with anyone who approaches you first. If you did not initiate the phone call or the contact, close your ears and close your mind to the story!**

I would include financial channel recommendations here, too. The greatest threat to your savings is a good story. If the deal were really a moneymaker, *no one would be telling you and me about it.* Hungry roosters don't cackle when they find a worm.

A few years back I was told of a former professional baseball player here in my hometown of Atlanta who'd had a long and lucrative career. He had big money and a marketable name—and no real investing savvy. He was approached by a developer during the home building boom. Induced (or seduced) to enter into a partnership with assurances that millions were lying on the ground for him and his new partner, he lost everything.

His "partner" overextended them, and when the housing market crashed, the banks came for their money. Somewhere in the mountain of papers this wealthy retired athlete had signed—papers he probably didn't understand—were provisions that made him personally responsible for the loans the developer had secured for the project.

He was shocked! He could have lived comfortably for the rest of his life even if he had never improved his financial position, but now he is broke. This man's earning capacity is long gone and the millions he had tucked away are now gone forever, too.

Learn from his misfortune and that of thousands of others with stories like his. When someone with an idea that had not occurred to you for "investing" your money approaches you . . . close your ears, close your mind, close your checkbook, and RUN THE OTHER WAY. Good deals never go begging for money; they are *kept away* from outside investors.

Some years back, I spent a few days on a privately owned, 16,000-acre hunting and fishing preserve. After a hunt, my host and I were sharing a drink and warming ourselves by a brisk fire in one of the lodges. This gentleman is by far the wealthiest man I have ever met. When our conversation turned to business he made a statement I will always remember. He said, "I have never put my money to work without complete control." He told me that since his first investment, he has never violated that self-imposed rule. No doubt his caution was a large part of his success.

I am not suggesting there can never be an exception, but this is one rule I intend to follow scrupulously and I urge you to do the same:

Limit your investments to situations you initiate, understand, and control.

That's how you avoid the really catastrophic loss.

A dear friend of mine received a lump sum retirement of one million dollars. As he was only in his fifties and would have to live on it for many years, he felt he had to find some way to grow it. Someone called and asked if he were interested in an oil and gas venture that looked promising. He agreed just to look and listen—his first mistake—and during the presentation he was sold on the groups past successes and convincing proposal.

Of course, he knew nothing of the business and certainly could not gauge the credibility of the claims, but the data they presented seemed overwhelmingly positive. In fact, they showed "proof" of success in twenty-three of their past twenty-four drilling ventures. He invested. The money was gone like smoke in the wind. Forever.

> Place a high value on certainty.
> —Benjamin Graham

He did not initiate the contact. He did not understand the business. He had zero control. The investment world is full of professional storytellers looking for people just like him. He told me later, "I should have been thinking about the fact that no more was coming so I had to protect what I had. Instead, I was only thinking I had to find some way to grow it. *I had it exactly backward.*"

There is as much wisdom as humor in Groucho Marx's quip, "The secret of life is honesty and fair dealing. If you can fake that, you've got it made."

Believe me, almost everyone can fake sincerity and integrity, but no one better than the hustler. Persuasive logic is his stock-in-trade. And it has never been any other way. Nearly three thousand years ago, a very wise king wrote these words: "The simple believes every word, but the prudent considers well his steps." (Proverbs 14:15, New King James Version) You will find that and a lot more wisdom about life in King Solomon's Book of Proverbs.

Keep your money safe from good stories and good storytellers. Hold it tightly until an opportunity is before you that no one needs to explain. You can give it to a professional manager of money with a reliable reputation and tell him you need five or six percent a year; you can buy rental property; you can hold the cash. But NEVER entrust your money to someone who approaches you first! If you did not initiate the contact, stay out of the deal!

Keep an Investment Journal

No judgment is needed when making regular deposits from paychecks into an investment account or when using a pro—both of which are good reasons to do it that way. But your personal judgment concerning investments that are speculative will benefit greatly from a written record of your thoughts.

Every time you enter an investment of opportunity—or seriously consider such an investment and pass on it—write down your reasoning in a computer file or a journal. Keep a written record of why you entered into and exited from each investment and record the profits or losses once it is closed. Include any relevant details. Why did you decide to buy or not to buy? Why did you make the decision to sell when you did?

Now, this is not so you can berate yourself over your past foolishness or gloat over your triumphs. It is to review so that the lessons you should learn don't slip away from you over time.

Your memory will not suffice. A written record will give insight into your weaknesses that an occasional mental review will overlook. As you review your journal from time to time, ask yourself questions like these:

- Am I speculating with too large a portion of my money?
- Am I jumping in and out of too many insignificant investments or am I doing it right and making purchases that have a real shot at doubling in value?
- Do I keep trying to catch the latest hot stock?
- Do I hurry into an investment because I fear I will miss profits if I wait to think through my decision thoroughly?
- Do I sell too early out of fear? Or too late out of greed?

- Am I investing only in situations that are so clear they "jump out" at me? Or am I constantly looking for something I think will make money and "reasoning" my way into the purchase—only to find out I was wrong because, in fact, no clear opportunity existed?

- Does my journal reflect decisions that respect how hard it was to earn and save that money? How easy it is to lose it? How hard it is to replace it?

As I've said before, investing intelligently is not a matter of becoming a money sophisticate. Intelligent investing is a plan and a set of rules you can understand and stick with. In my case, I buy the assets I have suggested when they are cheap since my free cash to invest with is irregular.

If I had a paycheck job, I would probably just set aside a percentage of my income every week and purchase stock funds at regular intervals. I would use any unexpected or extra money that came my way to accumulate toward buying a precious metals fund or a rental when gold was cheap or the real estate arrangement would work for my situation.

The small amount I set aside for reacting to special opportunities is a personal preference of mine. It has matured me—as a person and as an investor. And remember: regarding special opportunities, patience, not quantity, determines profits. Three or four such investments can be enough to justify a lifetime of waiting.

By the way, if you purchase an individual stock or commodity for a profitable trade (as opposed to a long-term hold), knowing a little about how to interpret a stock chart showing price and volume can help. You don't want to buy or sell something when everything about the chart's action is screaming to do the opposite. Why? Because a chart can show you what the crowd is doing wrong.

For example, I remember when a commodity rose 400 percent over two years and then spiked up wildly on monster volume, only to close in a sell-off at the lowest price of the day. That was an unmistakable signal that the big institutional money was selling out at that price and it was time to leave. You won't always get such a clear signal, but you should at least know what one is.

I am not a chart reader, but in some instances, just a working knowledge can give you valuable insight. The many books written by William J. O'Neil on chart analysis will be helpful here, but I am not suggesting chart reading should become the basis for your decisions or you should get caught up in the hype that if you learn to read a chart, you are going to make money that way.

In my opinion, chart reading is a helpful tool, but not something to live or die by with your money. So, if you read the books written by chart analysts, don't become enamored with the idea. You might just want to learn the clearest signs of accumulation and sell-offs.

After entering into an opportunistic investment, your thoughts will likely turn toward self-doubt. I find my journal benefits me most by calming me down and helping me stay the course when I am having second thoughts after my money is on the line.

It's to be expected that there will be some apprehension with any commitment of capital. When I make up my mind to enter into an investment if certain things happen . . . well, it is only natural to pause in those times when everything falls into place and wonder, "Did I overlook something?" Investing opportunities usually occur during periods of distress when bad news and fear are thick. There will be ambivalence until you mature from your own investing experiences to the point that you have complete confidence in what you are doing.

If I begin to doubt my decision once I've actually made an investment I will use my journal to review my rationale for the purchase in the first place. If nothing fundamental has changed, and if there are no abrupt drops in price on huge volume—which always means *sell*—the journal helps me quiet my concerns and stay the course.

Remember: it is important you do your thinking before you invest—and make a record of those thoughts—because, once you make an investment, the profit is made by sitting and letting things play out, not by constantly rehashing your decision, checking prices every day and second-guessing yourself. Every crop needs time to grow.

Review your journal whenever you begin to feel nervous. As long as you feel your initial reasoning is still valid, this review should strengthen and calm you. However, unless you are really unusual or already a confident investor, wide mood swings from optimism to grave doubts may occur from one hour to the next. A back-and-forth swing from confidence to anxiety is normal and to be expected with new investors. It was the same way when you first started riding a bike, wasn't it?

Speaking from experience, the apprehension eventually goes away. Once you have learned to wait until the buy price alone is such a bargain that it compels you to act, *and* you know you can hold on for a long time if need be . . . well, there will not be much in the way of nerves.

I do have one strong caution: if the price falls sharply after your purchase for reasons you do not understand, then sell quickly and recover what you can. You have probably made a mistake. By the time the reasons for the price falling sharply are clear, it will be too late to recover. *This is the only rule that is never wrong, no matter what happens afterward.*

Actually, if the investment under consideration is a stock or commodity, it might be wise to put a stop-loss order under it when you buy, so it will be sold automatically if the price falls by more than you would be comfortable with.

Remember this rule, as every experienced speculator who has ever made a dime preaches it:

The first loss is the cheapest loss.

If you make a speculative stock or commodity investment for a profitable resell, and the price starts falling sharply on big volume after you buy—SELL! Never sit and hope for a turnaround while looking right at the "big hit" happening to *you*. Those numbers on the computer screen or on your statement are real money.

I have made investments that declined ten percent after I bought them, but not precipitously on big volume, and they turned around and did well. I have also done the opposite: watched an investment lurch downward ten percent, and much more, on big volume and done nothing because I did not want to admit my mistake and take such a quick loss of several thousand dollars. That will prove the costliest thing you ever do if you don't learn from my mistakes.

I accrued foolish, needless, large losses that bothered me for years because I refused to admit my error when I had the first clear warning, but I have never had more than a few days' mild irritation over selling to protect myself and then seeing the price advance afterward. The pain from taking a big loss stays with you for years. The disappointment from a missed opportunity goes away quickly.

When you are wrong, admit it at the first clear warning and recover what you can.

When I enter an opportunistic investment, I will decide on one of two courses ahead of time:

1. I will not sell if the price falls after I buy it. I got my price and I know this will turn out well in the long

run. Though I don't know what will happen short term (it may go down more for a while), this is right long-term and I will wait it out.

I bought my first gold at $437 an ounce and it declined to around $385 right afterward. I did not sell. I knew I was right long term. This was a case of holding no matter what, made easier by the fact that I was buying gold and not a stock, as there was no chance of some disastrous news like accounting fraud. I sold it ten years later and paid cash for a nice car for one of my daughters and used the rest for other investments.

2. Though my logic tells me this is right, I will sell if it turns against me by more than I am comfortable with, usually about ten percent. To be safe, I may put a stop-loss order in to sell automatically if the price drops to my maximum loss point.

I learned these two rules the hard way. Don't assume the preacher or professor or author you admire has it all together while you have a long way to go. Everyone looks bright behind a podium. I may have better judgment now, but it came from a lot of incredibly bad judgment.

If you are considering putting money on the line, may I suggest you reread this entire book on investing beforehand? I do it and I wrote the book. I think the best use of *Invest Like a Wealth Manager* is as a quick-read safety manual before putting money at risk. Reading it before investing is cheap insurance against making an irreversible blunder.

Of course, if you have the money to use a professional, as long as you both are on the same page, let him or her do their job. Two people can't drive the same car at the same time.

One More Time: Don't Get Greedy

Bernard Baruch wrote, "Once I thought it wise to sell, I did so. That is why I kept my fortune." This is similar to another bit of Baruch's wisdom I quoted in the last chapter, but the point he was making here is different: he followed his own judgment rather than opinions of crowds or commentators.

And we must, too. When we become special opportunity investors, you and I must learn to buy when we look like fools for buying and to sell when we look like fools for selling. The future looks great at the top, but the top is no place to be holding an investment. When everyone wants what you have, let them have it. And if you ever begin to think you must be an investment genius—*sell!*

> It is looking at losses that kill investors. It is best to wait until money is lying on the ground.
> —Jim Rogers

Know that mistakes will be made. If you deliberatively review your reasons for an investment and subsequent prices lead you to conclude an error was made or circumstances have changed, then an exit is warranted. Calmly exit. And, whether time proves you right or wrong, do not continue to second-guess your decision to enter or to exit. Recover what you can of your investment and move on from where you are then. You have done the best that you could. You are getting smarter. The case is closed.

And *do not* try to get your money back with another investment. That changes the equation from honest error to folly. Just close the books on it and reset the financial plan to where you are. The surest way to lose more money is secretly to be thinking about how to get back the money you just lost.

Remember: if you have followed my advice, you have not risked any more than ten to twenty percent of your investment capital. This being the case, even the total loss of the invested funds cannot do you irreparable harm.

MORE HARD-WON TIPS

And as I have said before, if you have no interest in opportunistic investment this money can be placed into long-term stock funds or added to your professionally managed account. Even though I have shared my reservations about having all your money in stocks or anything else, stock prices will climb over long periods of time, and holding on or adding during recessions is evidence of investment maturity—and emotionally easier to do when it isn't every dime you have.

When you close a losing investment, write down your reasons for closing it, and record your losses. If my experience is typical—and I suspect it is—the most common reasons for losses are

- making the mistake of thinking you can learn to make money by watching financial television channels or reading money magazines and then picking stocks with your new knowledge.

- making a speculative investment based on your own reasoning rather than being compelled by a crystal-clear opportunity that captured your attention on its own.

- getting impatient with money because you are too immature to accumulate capital *and do nothing with it, even for years at a time,* until a clearly safe and profitable opportunity jumps out at you.

- investing too much of your money after listening to a convincing pitch from someone who contacted you first.

- making an individual investment—a single stock, a speculative investment, etc.—with too large a percentage of your funds.

- trying to make money do too much.

About that last one? The best advice I ever got on this point came from a wealthy friend and counselor—though I had to lose a lot before I appreciated his wisdom.

He told me, "When I was trying to make money all I got for it was a lot of loss carry-forwards to report on my tax return. I never made any money until I quit trying to make it and started trying not to lose it."

Money will run from any man or woman who fidgets with it too much or whips it too hard.

Remember: writing words on paper does not make any author an expert. I cannot tell you how hard it was for me to learn to avoid these common errors. A journal has helped, but no one is immune to human emotions. And we all start inexperienced and unsure.

The important thing is that you do not keep making the same mistakes over and over.

One final bit of advice: if you don't have enough cash in a savings account to replace your income for three to six months in the event of emergency, then you don't need any plan other than to save that much. You must start there. The most important investment is to build up a healthy reserve of cash to fall back on.

If you struggle to save a few thousand dollars in a year, then you don't need to be thinking about investing and diversifying yet. The amount to work with is simply too small. Truthfully, to arrange any meaningful multiple asset allocation plan, you need a base of maybe $50,000 or so. To use a professional wealth manager, you will probably need a couple of hundred thousand. Any less makes diversification impractical.

Finally, if you are frustrated by your current income or the life path you are on, then you might want to read my fourth book, *Unchain Your Brain*. It is about making positive changes in your life.

CHAPTER 9
WISDOM KEYS

The suggestion that everyone should be investing their money is as invalid as the advice that everyone should go to college.

There seems to be so much to know in order to invest like a wealth manager. But most of that wisdom can be distilled into the following collection of short items, each one a guidepost for intelligent investing with peace of mind.

Don't worry about remembering everything. Just skim through these bits and pieces before investing to keep your money safe.

- If you're not sure what to do, or if the subject of investing makes you feel nervous and overwhelmed, just hold on to your cash.

  Why do I say that? Think about it this way: you didn't go to work in order to invest, did you? Not likely. I didn't either. We go to work to earn, and hopefully to save, some money. And, if you now have your bills paid and have saved some of the money you worked for, then you have right now exactly what you went after.

If keeping that cash gives you mental comfort and investing it makes you anxious about what may happen to it in the future, why go from mental peace to stress? The first benefit of having earned and saved money is your own peace of mind. The suggestion that everyone should be investing their money is as invalid as the advice that everyone should go to college.

My mother never could look at a monthly investment statement without being worried in the months the investments decreased in value, so she decided to sell and just hold on to her cash. And she lives a more peaceful life because of it.

The two greatest investments I ever made were tithing and paying off creditors. Why? There was no risk of loss with either one, there was no way to go wrong when I did it, it added more to my peace of mind than any other investment ever has—and it pays dividends for life.

- If you do decide to invest, keep it simple by taking whichever of the following courses suits you best:
    - Invest regularly out of each paycheck and do not stop when prices go down.
    - Invest for the long term, but only enter an investment when prices are depressed. Refuse to be bothered if prices go lower still. You got your price; forget about it afterward.
    - If you occasionally come into some extra money, you might want to spread it around a bit beyond stock funds when prices are favorable.
- Don't bounce from one idea to another. The one thing fatal to all investment is constantly changing your method. There are many ways to invest, but

none work if you are running back and forth like a dog chasing a ball.

Remember my modest neighbor's wise point of view:

> I would watch investment shows and notice that even the experts couldn't agree from week to the next, and I know they are smarter than me. So, I just followed my own simple plan for thirty years and ignored all the ups and downs. My wife and I lived within our means and when I reached retirement age—I actually could retire.

- Once you have enough money to qualify, and especially if you come into money, you may want to consider a professional investment manager with a tactical plan for protecting accounts in the volatile world of money, markets, and interest rates. They understand a broader range of options, make decisions for you based on rules they understand and abide by, and have no emotional involvement.

  When choosing this person, get references from someone of wealth who has a long history with the money manager and can vouch for his or her character and methods.

- Hold some of your savings in cash for emergencies. And, only if you are inclined to do so, hold a little extra cash for an unanticipated opportunity of an exceptionally clear nature.

  I say again: do not look for these opportunities. If you do, you will trick yourself into taking action when nothing is there. Wait until you are minding your own business and something just grabs your attention. Two or three of these investments in a lifetime is all you need to make a big difference.

- Trading in and out of positions is reserved for experts. And very few people are experts. I am not an expert, and it is unlikely that you are.

If I invest ten percent of what I have saved into an opportunistic investment, I am not being a trader. I am picking up something of value someone else threw on the ground in a panic. I will hold that item until some normalcy resumes in its value and then, if I choose, sell it.

- The majority of your money and mine will not be made from investing, but will come from what we do for a living and what we can save over a lifetime. The purpose of investment is to grow our savings; not to put everything we have gained at risk chasing the big payoff. Maybe two or three times in a lifetime an unexpected opportunity offers us an above average boost.

> Don't feel the need to do anything with your money unless you are *more comfortable* with that than just holding on to your cash.

Investing, with only rare exceptions, is a business of growth over decades. When we adjust our "what should I be doing with my money" to that reality, we have made a giant step forward in maturity and safety. This mindset also makes it easier to avoid being seduced by financial publications and television shows promising "big profit" ideas.

Nothing you do in the investment world with your extra money is likely to make you rich, but there are a lot of things that can make you poorer. I have covered most of them in this book.

Financial independence comes from eliminating and avoiding consumer debt and the discipline to save a portion of each paycheck. Wealth is the result of becoming successful in business or in some form of profitable dealings. If you start thinking some shrewd investment can become a substitute for those things—you are walking onto thin ice.

I suggest you get off the wealth-chasing merry-go-round so many of the financial channels and magazines peddle. Instead, follow a simple written plan, read to improve your knowledge and character, walk through larger doors when they are opened to you, be open to take what life gives you in the way of new opportunities, and when you see none, *respect your cash.*

If you will keep your focus on improving yourself and your income that will make you a lot happier and a lot more money than constantly fiddling with investments.

- Intelligent investing is not a series of brilliant money moves. It is a sensible plan that will allow you to improve your position and live free from a grasping preoccupation with money. A professional manager, if one has enough to qualify, makes that process even easier.

- Writers of books on investing in real estate and stocks imply that just as they invested their way to wealth, you can learn to as well. I am sure that for them, it is true. But if after reading their books you get enthused, I think you should be on guard against taking too much on yourself right away. They entered that activity as a business and had a flair for it. But few have that flair. Trying to duplicate their results with much, or all, of the money you have will likely end badly. Certainly, grow in knowledge and skills, but don't dive into new ventures headfirst. Learn to swim in shallow water.

I applaud the men and women who share their knowledge to improve life for the rest of us. I do not discourage anyone from reading such books. I have read many and benefited much. But never bet the farm on a new venture. *Invest Like a Wealth Manager* will allow you grow in financial savvy and protect your money from inexperience, naïveté, promotions, and deceptions.

- You went to work to provide a living for yourself and save some cash. So don't feel the need to do anything with your money unless you are *more comfortable* with that than just holding on to your cash. For example, if I had a job, I would be a lot more comfortable investing a portion out of each paycheck into stock funds for thirty years than holding on to that cash in a bank and hoping inflation would go away. And I might invest occasionally in some assets besides stocks when there was a sale on, just to be safe.

    Do you see what I mean? Intelligent investing is not hard for any of us if we will stop trying to think like new money moguls and just go back to being "us" with our money. And if a wealthy friend in whom I had confidence recommended a professional manager, once I had the money to qualify, I would be more comfortable with that professional working to protect my investments than just putting my money on the waves of the market for my remaining investment years.

    Again, do you see what I mean? Do not assume you need to learn something new or complicated. Just use your own common sense and decide what *you* are most comfortable doing, considering your own circumstances at the time. And you can adjust your plan to suit yourself as the circumstances of your life change.

The long-term protection of capital is the top priority of the sober-minded investor, not gambling to become richer. As quoted earlier, Warren Buffet, perhaps the greatest investor of modern times, said, "Even to make large amounts of money, I will not do anything that is a risk to capital." You and I would do well to make that sentence the foundation of our thinking when it comes to our own money.

- Here is the only thing you and I need to do to act like a pro: have a sensible plan that will work *over time* and follow it.

  If your wealth increases and you can diversify investments or upgrade your overall plan with professional guidance, fine. But don't spend your life preoccupied with wealth and investing. You will probably put your money in harm's way if you do and spend way too much time preoccupied with money while the more valuable things of life slip by.

- Keep it simple. Get out of debt and save some cash. Buy some stock funds. Pick up a little gold and silver when precious metals are out of favor. If your means and lifestyle ever allow it, buy a rental or something else that will give you some cash flow. (Personally, I think rental income is the best investment of all. I pay cash or close to cash, so there is no risk of over-leverage. But for the average wage earner that is not possible. The recommendation to buy multiple rental properties can put them in a position of over-reaching or be too impractical for their income.)

And if you cannot do some aspect of that comfortably, leave it alone and don't lose any sleep over it. Stay on course with the parts you can do comfortably.

- Even if you can save very little, it is not likely you will ever go without food and shelter for a single day of your life. So if you cannot save or invest right now, do not let it depress you. Don't be discouraged by it. We have all been there. And please do not be talking and thinking LACK, even if it happens to be your temporary condition. Fear and discontent only attract more lack. Gratitude, even if only for your job and health, enlarges and attracts more of every good thing.

- Consider this if you have no money to invest: a side business paying you just $500 a month that you put into the bank is like having $120,000 invested at 5 percent interest. You can do that! And this is big: a side business can be more valuable than any investment you will ever make. If you want to increase your wealth, it makes a lot more sense to think about how you can do your job $500 a month better, or start that side business, rather than pondering how to drive your investment dollars into the stratosphere.

- What you do for a living is by far your most important financial investment. So, if all you do after reading this book is:
    - get out of debt
    - split any extra money between a little cash to cover you for a few months and make regular investments into stock funds
    - ignore the ups and downs of the world's economies and trials

- enjoy your life and your family—

You *have* a good plan for your money. And one that leaves plenty of room for the truly valuable things far more important. This book shares with you other options, but you need not take any if you are not inclined.

- Obsessing over investment profits is behaving like the dog at the greyhound track always outrun by the mechanical rabbit. If you allow it, money will run your life while giving you less and less in return.

- How foolish. You can only buy a bed so soft, and even steak loses its appeal if eaten too often.

> *How much do we really need to be happy?*
> *I can tell you with certainty,*
> *it is far less than we think.*

Our physical life on this earth is brief, and money's main benefit is to allow us to enjoy the four things that truly matter:

1. Family
2. Friends
3. Fun
4. Faith

You can make those things expensive, but you don't have to. Those four things, not money, are the true riches of life—and what will matter the most when you die. If money is separating you from them, then *you are paying too much for money.* You can pay too much for anything. Even money can become too expensive.

After securing your basic needs and comforts, money's real value diminishes. This world's cravings for more are inexhaustible. At some point you must learn to look away.

- As your income rises, set up mental barriers to avoid the subtle trap of being lured into purchases that result in a greater loss of time and freedom. The purchase price is only the beginning of the cost of a thing. The amount of your life it takes to maintain it and manage it is the real cost. Make a decision ahead of time not to desire rewards that have to be attended to and maintained. The quality of our financial health is determined by acquiring the things that are truly needed and refusing to put a high priority on acquiring additional things we can do without. Purchases that require support and maintenance are for the truly wealthy.

- It might be wise to reread *Invest Like a Wealth Manager* before you make any major investment decision. That three-hour investment of time can increase your confidence that what you are about to do is prudent and all but eliminate the possibility of doing something you may have real reason to regret.

One More Thing: Stewardship

This bit of wisdom, if I may claim to have any, deserves its own section. And I start by asking: does greater wealth include a responsibility to use it well?

As a Christian, my answer is yes. But, if there were no God and I could only consider the question from my personal observations of who is really happy, I would come to the same conclusion.

As I see it, God gave me the talents and health and opportunities with which I earn any wealth I've accumulated, so he has the right to ask me to use some of it to help his other children who are not so fortunate.

Let me explain through a couple of personal examples. I recently bought a new pickup truck. Now when I buy a truck, I have no emotional attachment to it. It's a tool to help me in my work. I will throw firewood or equipment in it five minutes after buying it.

But not long after that particular purchase, I decided I would make a surprise gift of the new truck to my daughter Sierra when she started driving in a couple of years. It then became important to me that there be no dents or scratches on the truck. I wanted to present it to her in good condition. I went from being the *owner* of a pickup to being the temporary *steward* of my daughter's truck. That meant that I was going to be more careful with it.

Well, when God entrusts money to us—particularly when it's more than we need to survive—we have no right to be careless with it, to give it our affection, or to lose it impetuously to our greed for more gain. We are to protect it, and to grow it when that can be done safely. We are custodians of the money.

It is the same as borrowing someone's car. You will drive a car that is on loan from a friend much more safely than your own if you feel any sense of gratitude and respect for the trust shown you.

If God answers our prayers and gives us much more than we need, is it unfair of Him if He asks us to give a portion of it to help someone else occasionally?

Let me give you a couple of examples. After meeting a single mother with three children, one of whom had special needs, and she with only a minimal income, my wife and I felt impressed to assist her in giving her children a good Christmas that year. We have kept that up throughout the many years since. In another instance, while driving to work one morning I was praying for a student in my daughter's school who had sickle cell anemia. I had never met or seen her and knew nothing about her other than hearing that a child in my daughters school had the illness and it was making school difficult for her.

Unexpectedly, as I prayed, I "felt" or "heard" these exact words come into my mind: "Mark, she has never had $1,000 of her own. Take $1,000 of My money and give it to her." Those very words came clearly to me, and they were not my thoughts. But here is my stewardship point: I felt so honored that God would refer to the money I had as His money that I got a little emotional. That meant He trusted me with money and we were in a partnership, He as provider and myself as trusted steward.

Now please don't think too highly of me. I share this only to explain financial stewardship. Had God said, "Give her $100,000," I probably would have cried a whole lot more—and for a very different reason!

But that free, open, trusting relationship of readiness for "call and response" is stewardship. God has blessed me with whatever I have. And I endeavor to be neither careless with it nor overly attached to it. It is His provision for my family, and if He gives me a surplus and calls for some of it to help someone else, I stand ready to obey as proof of my gratitude—and to demonstrate that I can be trusted with more.

My wife, who is far wiser than I, spontaneously wrote this down for me in less than three minutes when I asked her to help me explain success to readers of my books:

> Success is not something in the future. Success is being in God's flow and purpose for your life, and out of that is a continuous current of blessing to us and through us.

Success is a life-giving river that runs through us. It is never stagnant, but always flowing and enlarging our influence for good. Money is just an automatic benefit that keeps this circle of good moving.

Success can be chosen at any moment without any additional attainments by just stepping into and trusting in that flow, being ready to give and receive with equal joy, being expectant of good, and releasing control of how it will happen. That river will do the work as long as we stay on the positive side of the flow and refuse the negative.

It is being ready to respond to the voice of the Divine Mind with an expectation of good for all. That is success.

My wife, Tracy, is a compelling example of what it should mean when someone says, "I believe in God."

How Will You Die?

Anxiety over lack of money can choke the joy of living right out of us. But so can a preoccupation with wealth and investing.

That is why I now recommend professionals, if one has enough assets so it makes sense. Conversations with a certified financial planner and a seasoned, tactical wealth manager—once you have a reasonable amount to protect and invest—are strong barriers against an inordinate preoccupation with money which some struggle with.

Not one man or woman in all of human history has ever died wishing they had spent more time with money. But a great many deeply regret that they spent too little time with the true riches of family, friends, and faith.

By all means, be productive. Be a good steward and use your talents. But invest regular quality time having fun with family and friends, and nurture your relationship with God. Money is important but use it in service to these things that are more excellent. That's the best asset allocation decision for real wealth building you will ever make.

CHAPTER 10
PLAY LIFE TO WIN, PLAY MONEY NOT TO LOSE

During a conversation with a very wealthy friend, I asked him to tell me which rule about handling money was his most important. He said, "I take as much time as I need in order to make sure that what I am doing is right and I am not making a mistake. If the deal is lost because of the time I took to reach my decision—and it sometimes is—that is the cost of doing business properly."

This man was born into a wealthy southern family, true gentry, but he wanted to make his own way. He had an interest in real estate and became wealthy in his own right acquiring it. He was cautious, and shrewd enough to know that his own desire for gain could rush him into a bad deal. But here is the main takeaway: he played life to win his own victories although he could have taken a first-class meal ticket. But when it came to investing his money, he invested his money *not to lose it*. He had it right:

> Play life to win; and play money not to lose.

Courage to Live without Regret

The Top Five Regrets of the Dying, written by former hospice caregiver, Bronnie Ware, is an insightful book that birthed real courage in me. She said the number one regret of the dying was that they didn't listen to and trust their inner voice and act on it. In other words, they regretted above all else that they did not step out boldly on that inner vision during the life they were given.

You do not want to come to the end of your life having ignored that inner voice. For me, my books are a result of listening to that inner voice, though the thought and the odds seemed sheer folly.

Don't live your life not to lose. If during your lifetime you "feel" a nudge that will not go away, listen to it. Life should be played to win. But most people play life not to lose; to avoid defeat, staying in the shallow end, in their comfort zone, where things look more controllable—all while investing money trying to "win big." *That is the losing side of both transactions.*

We are put here, I believe, because we have things of significance to do and paths of faith to walk: difficulties to overcome, lessons to learn, growth to achieve, skills to gain and, in time, strengths to share. Our best life *is* on that high road. Fulfilling our true potential takes a certain amount of courage. Life should not be feared and played not to lose.

New challenges are how we grow, and mistakes are how we learn, and that inner voice helps us live our lives with meaning and purpose. This is not a suggestion to act rashly, but an observation that, if a bigger door opens, action almost always beats inaction. But, when it comes to money, saved money should be protected.

So, if you find a home you can rent for more than the payment, that is a safe move—even if it makes you nervous because you are new at it. But that is playing the money game not to lose because the arrangements are sensible.

However, if you buy something that will take every dime you can scrape together because you think you can sell it later for more than you paid for it, you are playing the game of money to win bigger than your means, and *that is unsafe.*

PLAY LIFE TO WIN, PLAY MONEY NOT TO LOSE

With money, playing safe is playing to win, but with your life, you will regret it if you make decisions with that same logic. Like a rubber band, you are made to stretch.

If something inside keeps giving you a nudge, you should follow your heart despite the unknowns. It was placed in my heart to write this series of books that covers the major issues of life; I heard that inner voice. And I heard it relentlessly.

My rational mind told me the very idea was ridiculous. I could not write, knew nothing about it, had no interest in it, and besides, the odds against success after all the effort were a million to one (which they still are). I would never invest money against those odds, yet I have put more than fourteen years of my life and spent tens of thousands of dollars into what you are reading now. But I felt something calling me from deep inside. And so, I am taking my shot at winning a life that is more than repairing houses, as honorable as that is.

If you ever hear a similar voice and it won't go away, step toward it. It is leading you to your destiny. My mother told me, "Son, if you listen to all the reasons why something can't be done, *you'll never do anything.*"

Safeguarding Your Money and Your Life

When you play life to win and money not to lose, you need to protect both, and there are some very specific, commonsense, practical ways to do that.

For one thing, I have insurance policies with enough umbrella coverage to withstand quite a storm.

For another, my assets are protected within an incorporated business or limited liability companies, all of which I manage. Personally, I own very little. These entities allow me some control over my income and expenses for tax purposes and separate my business affairs so one incident cannot expose everything else I have to a lawsuit.

It is usually not wise to build things of value and keep them in your own name; everything you have is fair game in litigation. When you are in debt and working for a paycheck, you are not as concerned about such things. But once you have something to lose, it is time to think about asset protection.

As your business interests or finances begin to grow, you will need professional counsel. If you are going to start a business or buy real estate, pay for an hour of professional guidance ahead of time to determine the legal entity that will provide the best protection and allow you to take full advantage of beneficial tax laws.

When I am going to do anything that produces income—including marketing these books—I consult with my attorney to determine the most beneficial way to go about it. I recommend you choose a successful law firm with in-house attorneys who specialize in real estate, tax strategy, asset protection, and estate planning. In fact, I always use specialist lawyers, as does any forward-thinking man or woman who wishes to protect what they have worked so hard to build.

In addition to legal counsel, always consult your certified public accountant (CPA) and perhaps, a certified financial planner (CFP). Keep your CPA informed before making any changes. It is imperative your business entities, asset protection strategies, wills or living trusts and other estate planning, are properly coordinated.

Some real estate investing courses offer classes on asset protection for a few thousand dollars. This becomes a very important subject when you have tenants. These instructive courses cover a lot more than just real estate and are well worth the money.

This type of knowledge is very specialized and changes as often as Congress modifies the tax code, but it is not something that should overwhelm you. When you have questions, just spend an hour with the law firm and CPA of your choice. Don't try to act smarter or richer than you are; just be yourself, briefly explain your intentions, and ask how to go about doing what you intend to do.

You should be willing to pay for the knowledge and help of experts as your business affairs grow. And some brokerage firms provide the services of a trained wealth management pro for free to their clients.

In Summary

Let me highlight some of the things I've learned that have helped me—and can help you—to think like a paid manager of your own wealth.

Get out of debt. During those years you are eliminating debts, read books on the subject of personal character and money.

Why character? Because it takes strong hands to hold a full cup. Here is a partial list of character deficiencies that can ruin years of effort: dishonest dealings, greed, marital infidelity, an ungoverned sex drive, drug use and overindulgence in alcohol. (Overcoming these pitfalls, so common to our human nature and so fatal to our plans, is discussed in my fifth and final book, *Private Choices, Public Power.*)

Make it a central part of your investment plan to get out of all consumer debt **ahead of schedule**.

Keep your investment money safe from salespeople and promoters. Don't be a typical "investor" chasing one high-flying stock after another. Have a simple investment plan that suits your temperament and skill level. This will accomplish much more for you than trying to hit one moving target after another with no overall plan for how your money will be allocated.

Allocate predetermined percentages of your income into universally valued assets, including some held in cash. There is no substitute for ready money. In addition to stocks—which should be bought on declines or at regular intervals out of your earnings—buy a little gold and silver when the prices retreat.

This will usually happen when the stock market is hot, and no one wants gold because the "smart money" is in the market.

If it suits your circumstances and your means, use a portion of your funds to buy a bit of real estate. If you do, keep the size of the payment within your ability to cover it for a while if it becomes necessary.

If your assets grow, you could add bonds or bond funds or limited liability partnerships (see Appendix 2) that have been professionally evaluated for suitability and safety, if you are using a professional with a tactical plan.

If it appeals to you, you might also want to consider being patient and completely inactive with 10 percent of your investment funds in order to take advantage of unexpected opportunities.

If you hold some money for special opportunities, do not be overactive. Two or three very clear opportunistic investments are enough for a lifetime. The most important three rules for this kind of investment are

1. Never do anything with this money as a result of someone approaching you first with a great investment.

2. Don't get impatient after years of holding cash.

3. Do not actively look for these opportunities. Let them be the ones that are so clear they jump out at you.

Have a plan and follow it. Money doesn't like being fiddled with!

Your job or career is about earning money; investing is about protecting what you have set aside from inflation and greed.

PLAY LIFE TO WIN, PLAY MONEY NOT TO LOSE

If you think at all about needing more money, think about earning more of it, not how to make what you already have produce ever-greater returns. In addition to being a waste of your time, money has a way of leaving when someone disturbs it too much.

This is another reason a professional can be such a beneficial part of your long-term success: constant vigilance and proven metrics for making adjustments are their full-time business.

Our life is not about money; it is about family, friends, fun with loved ones, and our faith. Money's purpose is to facilitate time for those things, not push them away and into the background. No book (including this one) ever written is going to turn you or me into a couple of investment gurus. One is either born with that faculty or not. So follow a simple plan: invest in widely held asset classes out of each paycheck or on declines. Ignore temporary ups and downs and keep your attention on improving your income from what you do for a living. If you ever come into money or save more than a couple of hundred thousand (2020 dollars) and it seems better to you, consult a professional.

One more time: if something on your investment list falls out of favor and is thrown overboard, rather than panic with the crowd, you might buy a little more of it if you have the ready money. Otherwise, keep your mind off the world's parade of financial traumas and dramas. As your means increase, let the world's financial crises become your opportunities as you pick up the bargains. This transfer of wealth during a crisis has been going on for all of human history. "Fools make feasts and wise men eat them," as our friend Ben Franklin says.

I cannot say this too often: *if a sincere and believable person approaches you with a good investment story, say, "No, thanks," and close your mind to it.* Bernard Baruch, perhaps the wealthiest investor of his day, made it a point to tell friends, "If you are about to give me a tip or a bit of inside information, please don't."

Never invest money with anyone who approaches you first. Never. Never invest in something you are unfamiliar with. Do not put yourself into a position where you can lose all your money if a second party does not perform up to their promises.

Do not let "friends" and relatives mistake you for a bank. You are not a bailout for others follies. Besides, it won't help them. It *will* prevent them from learning their own lessons, regardless of what they promise you, and once you let it start there is no end until you are just as broke as they are—and twice as foolish. They need to learn their own lessons in life. Your interference will harm you both.

Protect your assets. Do not hold all your assets or even significant amounts of money in your own name. As your wealth increases and diversifies, consult a law firm with specialists in asset protection and estate planning and/or a certified financial planner. Attorneys who specialize in these areas of law, and men and women who have achieved the CFP designation, can help us be prepared for a host of potentialities we would never even think of.

Have reasonable expectations. Stop thinking that there is some secret out there that is going to allow you to turn $5,000 into $100,000. The number of men and women who can invest excess capital over a long number of years and through the constant changes in economic conditions, and consistently achieve life-changing returns after the inevitable errors in judgment, inflation, taxes, and external events beyond their control, is infinitesimally small. And this includes the highest-paid professionals on Wall Street. To consistently make investment decisions that exceed the *real* rate of inflation is so difficult that it is an anomaly even on Wall Street.

I am well aware of the high rates of return touted by the writers of real estate investment books. But I wonder just how many real estate investors were prepared for the sudden collapse of real estate prices, the complete dry-up of available capital for potential buyers, and the flood of vacant rentals and commercial space that happened worldwide beginning in 2008?

Those high returns on invested capital are only possible when the leverage rate (debt to equity ratio) is very high. Most of those people got wiped out in the most recent global real estate meltdown.

Bottom line: there is no surefire method to investing your way to wealth. To compensate for this reality, I will endeavor to use my few extra dollars to spread the strongest and broadest net possible under me using methods I understand—and have now shared with you.

Frankly, I am behind the curve. Why? Because everything I have written I learned from first doing it the wrong way myself. Years later, my consolation is the knowledge that this useful book, and all the others in the Common Sense for a Prosperous Life series, would never have been possible otherwise.

From my errors I have learned the only control available to me is to buy a few universally valued assets when the buy price makes it compelling and ignore all the stories of how someone else made a fortune last year. A professional who has a reputation for honesty and capital preservation, who manages money tactically and stands ready to protect accounts during market declines with contrarian positions, who has a defensive strategy to hold account values near neutral—or even profit from bear strategies in the event of a sudden global crisis—who is ready to adjust to moves in interest rates . . . is a great ally when one has enough saved to put him or her to work.

My Story Can Be Yours

I went to work for myself, part-time at first, to see if I could improve my future. I was determined to pay off my debts with any money I could gain from the enterprise because, frankly, I had little confidence I would prove capable over the long haul. But as I have said, when an opportunity to move ahead is presented, action almost always trumps inaction, whether one is confident or not.

I persisted because my hunger to escape a life in which every dollar had to be weighed before being spent was great. I set aside some cash for emergencies, and later, once out of debt (the work of many, many years), set aside enough money to cover the next year's major expenses as a buffer. I have not always been able to maintain that, but I do as much toward it as I can each year. Then—not all at once, but as I could afford it—I bought a rental home and a few other assets.

And along the way, I made distressing mistakes of every sort, which I now see were part of a beneficial plan for my life—a plan that resulted in my writing five to-the-point books loaded with real-life lessons.

If my writings sell (and they will!), I'll take the proceeds and repeat the process outlined in this book. Doing it better this time. Learning from the wisest of the three little pigs, I am cobbling together a house made of brick—one brick at a time. If you can do it faster or better, God bless you.

Even men and women who succeed in building businesses of their own have no real advantage in knowing what to do with the excess capital their business provides. That's why the best investment I ever made had nothing to do with investing money. It was my decision to find a way to work for myself, and then stick with it until I found a way to make the business work. (The many valuable and hard-won lessons I learned about starting and running a business are in my third book, *The Entry-Level CEO*.)

By the way, the second-best investment I ever made was to get completely out of debt and to own my home outright.

A business you are good at or a career path you enjoy will trump any investment plan on earth when it comes to securing your future. Keep your focus on caring for the goose that lays the eggs, not on counting the eggs. As my wife said, "You have to take good care of whatever takes care of you."

Thankfully, being a man or woman of financial sophistication is not necessary. Steve Forbes, of *Forbes* magazine fame, candidly admitted in a televised interview that his famous grandfather told him, "Steve, you can make a lot more money selling financial advice than following it."

Financial sophistication may not be necessary, but a little common sense definitely is. Perhaps a few thoughts in this book have put you on that path. The suggestions offered in *Invest Like a Wealth Manager* will give you a solid foundation and a sensible guide for sound thinking concerning investment.

> *The only protection that will ever exist for capital is the common sense possessed by the controller of it.*

The Common Sense for a Prosperous Life series is a PHD level course in common sense applied to critical life subjects. Everything unnecessary has been swept away in my many read-throughs. There is no filler, no chitchat, no dribble. Truthfully, I find many books I have read should have been reduced to a few pages as the writer can hardly get to the point. Not here. My writings are distilled until the reader may open any of the books to any page and, within a few paragraphs, be receiving compelling information on a subject of great importance to him or her.

And why should I leave God out of my comments, if I feel the omission would be a disservice to the reader? It is my view that God created commerce and life and He has a Father's desire that we use our life well and enjoy it. And if I am wrong in those assumptions, I am certainly no worse off.

Question: are there more profitable things one can do with their money than what I have described in the previous pages? Absolutely. Many. *But the average person can actually do what I write about.*

And my books can be read in small doses to great benefit. I purposely separated my writings into short books, each covering only a few related topics. That way they make easy quick-reference manuals to carry with you. Keep handy the one most helpful to you at the time and read a few pages while waiting for your next appointment.

And occasionally, think about giving one of my books as a gift to someone who will benefit. Then, watch for the act of kindness to return to you. *Start the mysterious flow of success moving through you to get it started flowing to you. Shift your life into forward gear without effort by sowing generous words and deeds to others. Speak them about yourself to yourself, too.*

My writings on money and business and private life teach sensibility and responsibility. They are not a call for everybody to become rich. The biggest pile of money on earth will become ash in our mouth if we make it a god.

Let me share one more bit of wisdom with you: *money is always willing to leave you.* When you love it and give it first place, there is no reciprocation. Money is always willing to be disloyal to you. It always wants to become master or escape. That is why it takes strong hands to hold it, to keep it in its place. I have strengthened your hand to that purpose—but not for money to become your purpose.

Ambition is good, but our life must be about more than chasing dollars. I can tell you from experience that fretting and straining over "What else should I be doing?" and "How can I make something happen with these dollars?" is not going to help you move forward financially at all. *Not one inch.*

So put all that mental straining to rest. Life is so much better after we give ourselves permission to enjoy the blessings we have right now and just trust the One arranging today to guide us into tomorrow. Quit making everything about future results. Let go of trying to control how everything in your life happens.

I believe this book has been sent to you rather than purchased. Maybe not even to learn more about money, but to change the way you think of it. Although grasping and desperation is fruitless, it is a fact that you *were* Made for More—so Make Room for it, be open for the right thought, or introduction, or connection. And the One who made you knows what that "more" is and how to get you there. (By the way, inviting God into your life can only help this entire process along.)

The call of God is always higher. Always. If we come to him, confessing our need of him, He will begin orchestrating everything else. With God as your partner, you won't have to be the one to figure everything out. That should be a load off.

I would never have guessed my struggles in business or my bitter follies with money were only to prepare me for my assignment of writing—a destiny I had never even had a remote suspicion of.

Perhaps you reading my books just now is no happenstance either. Are you hungry for something more? They say God parted the Red Sea with a stick. Isn't it reasonable to believe he can do more with your life and mine than we can? Let's ask him to.

Appendix 1:
THE TRUTH ABOUT INFLATION

Inflation is the consequence of printing more of a nation's currency out of thin air, resulting in a decrease in the value of the money in circulation. The decline in value we refer to as inflation is the result of *inflating* the supply of the unsupported currency. Hence the term "inflation."

The Founding Fathers of the United States intended this to be made impossible to the new federal government by stipulating that all money was to be supported by silver or gold. In such an economy, the dollars printed—not allowed to exceed a definite standard of value—are thereby made safe from government destruction, which takes place when inflation is used to cover overspending. If you can't print more money than you have, you can't destroy its value.

Such a protected economy would expand and contract without manipulation, reacting only to free-market forces, just as any living thing must breathe in and out. Today, every healthy contraction in economic activity, with its resulting correction in prices, is fought by inflating the currencies of the world further.

Why? Partially to satisfy voters who never want to have to deal with a healthy realignment to real values. And partially to devalue the currency, which makes government repayment of outstanding debts more affordable. A weak currency also facilitates exports, as our goods will then be more affordable to foreign buyers as their currency gets stronger relative to ours. It makes our goods cheaper to them.

These are all short-term, feel-good gains, but nothing is designed to survive if it never exhales. Eventually, the constantly reflated balloon must burst; the currency becomes ever less valuable—such as when the average price of a home or car or loaf of bread costs every new generation four times more than the previous generation had to pay—and the working-class population is in an increasingly desperate state. The middle-class begins to decline. The society becomes the working poor and the well-connected super rich.

If these simple economic lessons were explained from grade school on, it would be more difficult for a runaway federal government to commit this national theft of the value of our labor and savings. National debt is a threat to our paychecks and freedoms.

Appendix 2:
BONDS AND LIMITED PARTNERSHIPS

Bonds are viewed as another form of cash, but in truth, in an environment of rising interest rates, bonds will fall in value, sometimes a lot.

Bonds are more complicated than most people, myself included, understand. Bonds do have a place if you want to convert money earned by labor into income. And the effect of compounding interest over a period of decades is powerful. However, one should only purchase bonds or bond funds with professional guidance to avoid issues with insolvency risks.

I would also buy bonds in those rare instances that the yield exceeded anything I was likely to make elsewhere, provided I had been assured by my financial advisor that the issuer was unquestionably solvent.

Such circumstances occurred in the 1970s when yields went into the teens on high-grade bonds while then Federal Reserve Chairman Paul Volcker was battling inflation. This Fed action, combined with a suspicion of dollar weakness by foreign buyers of US debt, drove interest rates paid on solid bonds to unprecedented heights.

I recommend buying bonds only with the counsel of someone who understands them because insolvency risks for municipalities, states, and now even entire countries are becoming too serious for the uninformed to venture there without professional guidance.

All these warnings apply equally for limited partnerships. Unless a professional informs your decisions, stay clear of arrangements you are not competent to judge.

ABOUT THE AUTHOR

Mark Ashe is the owner of a successful home improvement business in Atlanta. He and his wife of over thirty years have three grown daughters. They enjoy life on their 40-acre farm in the rolling hills of north Georgia, traveling with friends or with their daughters, and great meals shared with close friends. Mark went from being a policeman to debt free and financially independent by his mid-forty's.

Mark writes and speaks with compelling clarity on "common sense for the uncommon life." A wealthy financial adviser has described Mark's writings as "a PhD level course in successful living."

Mark's premise, and the proof of his life, is that an average man or woman can attain surprising success when the desire to do so is strong and the major decisions of life are made with a practical sensibility that his books bring to life through personal examples.

Connect at www.markashe.com

www.ingramcontent.com/pod-product-compliance
Ingram Content Group UK Ltd.
Pitfield, Milton Keynes, MK11 3LW, UK
UKHW022237230426
12048UKWH00018BA/1312